NOTES FROM AFGHANISTAN

STEVEN SPECHT

IN RETROSPECT

I originally wrote this in the summer of 2012, shortly after returning from a year in Afghanistan. I suppose 2020 is a good year for hindsight. Eight years later, I see things I wish I had written better and perspectives that were short-sighted. Despite the urge to revise, I have made no changes. I give it to you, warts and all.

What I capture well is the scope of boredom that comes with being in a combat zone without technically being in combat. The letters to my parents and future wife on the mundane seem as interesting as watching the paint peel. It is by far the best takeaway.

What has not aged well is the sense of idealism that existed then, the idea that there was a path to a victory worthy of the blood and treasure. At 29, I pushed for a belief that we could "win" what has become our longest war. In reality, the evidence presented by the Washington Post reveals efforts by civilian leadership to hide the truth from the American public. What's one more parallel to the Vietnam Conflict but our very own Pentagon Papers?

If I and everyone like me was a rube who could not see the forest for the trees, the blame lies with the generals who did not speak up, or did not speak loud enough.

From my vantage point in 2012, I saw as far as I could.

Steve

NOTE TO READER

When deciding on transliteration, I have done my best to use the most common spellings. While many in the Islamic World would prefer the Muslim Holy Book to be called 'The Holy Quran,' Americans generally recognize it as the 'Koran,' so I have used that spelling. I use the alternative spelling 'Muhammad' to identify the Prophet in Islam, and 'Mohammad' as a key person in this narrative. For simplicity, I've used the 24-hour clock format. For those unaware of how to convert 1300-2400 to 'p.m.,' simply subtract twelve; 1630 becomes 4:30 p.m. Generally, I use the term 'coalition' when referring to the overall effort in Afghanistan. This is personal preference after years of reading and watching biased American media, which often downplays the efforts of the numerous countries. Many of which have given money, time, and personnel to the mission. At times I deviate from this standard to highlight the sacrifice of an individual country in a particularly bloody day such as, "...12 Turkish soldiers getting killed..." etc. I debated on the appropriate title for some time, but eventually settled with something simple. Strangely, I dwelled longest on the use of the preposition "from" rather than "on," for many of my observations extend to the Islamic world as a whole or circle back to life in America.

FOREWORD

While serving in the United States Air Force from 2006-2010, I had the good fortune to be a Pashto linguist. I attended the Defense Language Institute (DLI) in Monterey, California for 47 weeks of intellectually grueling coursework. The majority of our instructors were born in Afghanistan, but I found it interesting that they came in three separate waves of immigrants. The first wave was those who fled the Soviet occupation, the second, those who fled the civil war and the rise of the Taliban, and the third, those that fled the coalition occupation. I was desperate to get first-hand knowledge of a culture and country I'd spent uncountable hours studying, but after a series of deployments to Southwest Asia, I realized that I would never make it to Afghanistan in the Air Force and I pursued a job as a contract linguist for the military. A private company filled gaps in the military with civilians who were primarily Afghan-Americans, but there was a handful of former military as well. While I preferred something more actively involved in peacekeeping to a job that I knew would be very similar to my Air Force job, at least I would be in Afghanistan.

While deployed in Afghanistan from April 25, 2011 to May 14, 2012, took copious notes in a "daily 100 words," idea I received from journalist Chris Hedges. "If you write 100 words a day, that's over 36,000 words.—enough to start the foundation of a book." The unofficial motto of the military is "hurry up and wait," so at times I skip days on which nothing substantial happened. An attempt to capture the boredom that pervades some parts of the deployment appears only as uninspired writing. For days on end spent waiting for a convoy, a flight, or an assignment are generally cobbled into one final entry, rather than a repetition of the same daily entry of "waiting." In addition to the daily journals, I wrote larger essays on individual subjects and over 100 letters home to friends and family. Relevant material has been pieced together into a coherent representation of my time in *Notes from Afghanistan*.

Many of my journal entries attempt to capture the day-to-day happenings of a deployed experience. I worked and lived alongside Marines, Sailors, and Soldiers, so my experience was often similar to theirs, sans combat. For anyone who has not been there, I hope I have effectively captured this feeling—repetition and monotony peppered with action and heartache while finding whatever diversion possible to make the time pass more quickly.

A lot of the letters home were observations about culture, through the lens of someone who had a decent understanding of what was going on having spent so much time studying it. Some of them are filled with over-the-top morbid humor; some are personal; some are serious.

For better or worse, at no point did I see anything even approaching conflict. On a few occasions, I was "shot near," but an evening of harassment from a very poor shot is the closest I've come to a fight. I have, however, interviewed plenty of people to get a feel for how things really are, and I shared living space with three men whose days were numbered. I have done my best to capture their thoughts and ideas honestly.

I've only included a few Americans in the final draft as my most important interactions were with Afghans. I've found it necessary to change the names of some of the Americans and all of the Afghans in this writing, but there are no composite characters. I feel it's prudent of me to change the Americans' names. Al Qaeda and other international groups have demonstrated a desire and ability to "reach out and touch us," so I don't want to leave it to chance that information provided in this text could possibly be used as background information. Americans will be identified with a first name and military members are identified with rank or distinguishing duty and their first name. It is even more dangerous for Afghans who live in constant threat of being attacked for their association with American forces. Some of them have had their photos taken by Taliban sympathizers and have a bounty on their head. Others have man-

aged to maintain their anonymity. I don't dare threaten their lives with my writing. Afghans will be identified in the same manner—first name and rank if necessary.

Over time, most of the Afghans I dealt with on a daily basis developed an extreme respect and trust of an odd, bearded American who engaged them whenever possible.

There were some holdouts who resented my

presence along with all foreigners, and I address those as well. The text also outlines some of my activities in my spare time including English lessons for Afghan soldiers and workers as well as some my private antics, including bird watching and gardening. The bulk of my time outside of work was spent on English lessons with the Afghans, and therefore, the bulk of this book is on that subject.

Despite some critiques of government policy, I never seek to dishonor the American and/or coalition men and women who have been thrust into this conflict; I make no apologies for my unwavering support of these fine people to whom we all owe a debt of gratitude.

Without further ado, I present *Notes from Afghanistan*.

1

MAY

May 1st

I've been at Bagram Air Field (BAF) for approximately a week.

The level of activity is staggering; I'd guess there are close to 20,000 people here at any given time. While a major center of operations, Bagram is as far away from the war as one can be. With the exception of an occasional mortar from the mountains and stray landmines left over from the Soviets, there is no immediate danger. It's a great place for a morning run and there is a fair amount of shopping alongside a coffee shop, the Base Exchange (BX or PX for Post Exchange) and a series of Afghan shops selling scarves, jewelry, and other trinkets. A few days a week there is a semi-authentic Afghan bazaar selling goods on the edge of the base, just inside the gate. Af-ter 0800 the commotion on the main corridor, Disney Drive, fills the air with dust and makes that side of the installation quite unpleasant. Disney is the namesake of one of the earliest casualties in Afghanistan, SPC Jason Disney who was killed in a non-combat related incident. It is commonplace for facilities and roads to be named after casualties. It's a temporary memorial in that someday, we'll depart this country, and Disney will be long forgotten to some Afghan name for the same road, but in the mean-time, it means something to someone.

Our temporary residence is at Camp Warrior on the far side of the flight line and away from the dust and commotion along Disney Drive. We are stacked two-high in poorly lit, dusty, and crowded tent. Almost all of the residents are Afghan-American linguists, save me and a few other contractors passing through.

Every new arrival to the tent is sick. After a week of long hours at Ft Benning for pre-deployment training, two days of international flights through five countries, and a non-existent sleep cycle, it is assured that everyone succumbs to what would be a mere cold in America but much worse in Afghanistan, exacerbated by the filth of the temporary quarters and dust of daily winds. In books, it's called the "Kabul cough." The constant uprisings of yellow dirt soak the linings of the lungs, and any exertion re-sults in a dry non-productive cough. Eventually, with enough coughing, a lining of grit sloughs off the lungs and comes out but the cough never stops. Running seems the only way to temporarily alleviate the cough by clearing the lungs with heavy breathing, but it returns shortly thereafter. Sleep is nearly impossible between my own fits of coughing and the intermittent snorting and coughing coming from adjacent bunks—oh well.

It's amazing how many people they can cram into these tents. I'm sharing 1/4 of an acre of tent area with about 100 people. They've run out of beds, so people are sleeping in the makeshift mosque that the Muslim interpreters have set up. I'm doomed to a bed right next to the mosque, and while they pray silently, I always hear them rustling about. The fever seems to be passing, but I thought that yesterday too; I just lay here in 90-degree heat sweating off a 100-degree fever; it's not bad enough to go to the doc. I blew my nose so hard I pulled a muscle in my neck. That's a rare tal-ent.

I'm allegedly going to Herat for my assignment, and this is too good to be true. Herat is not only safe but also beautiful. I question the logic of this choice since my primary language is Pashto and that area of Afghanistan speaks only Dari. I'm sure this is a mistake on the part of the military but I can't do anything about it. As of now I don't have a flight. The worst-case scenario is that I arrive to Herat and I'm told that there is nothing for me. At least I'll have seen more of the country.

May 2nd

This base is absolutely beautiful. We are surrounded on three sides by mountains that I'd estimate to be 12,000 feet—small by Afghan standards where 19,000-foot peaks are common and the ceiling is just shy of 25,000 feet. There is a blanket of smog at times, but when the wind is right, it's an amazing view. Rain every few days ensures a lush green zone surrounding the base with agriculture; it also keeps the dust down for a day.

I went for a fair amount of exploring with a camera and binoculars. There is an endless amount of hassle from Security Forces, which detains me long enough to check my ID and paperwork before driving off without a word. Regardless of the hassle, there is no explicit rule against photography beyond the restriction on flight line photography. Stateside I'm an avid bird watcher and a mediocre photographer, so I'm hoping to continue that habit here. So far I have about seven species but I'm frustrated that most of these common species are ones that have been introduced to Amer-ica as exotic, invasive species, so they are nothing new for me to see. The most inter-esting thing so far was a House Sparrow caught in concertina wire, pinned there by a Turkestan Shrike, a bird of prey, that frequents the fields alongside the fence. Today I'm going on a run on the ring road which is about 8 miles long by my estimation. It's a neat historical route past a bunch of old Soviet bunkers and bomb storage facilities that are in complete disrepair. There are also a lot of old blown up vehicles out that way from an unknown era. None of them are coalition vehicles, as far as I can tell.

The area alongside the road is roped off because of land mines and other unexploded ordinance. As is the case everywhere, here there are teams from Africa mine sweeping, but they only get a few hundred a day according to the gentleman from Zimbabwe I spoke with yesterday. The estimate on the amount of unexploded ordinance (UXO) in Afghanistan runs anywhere from half a million to 10 million*. It's relatively com-mon to see Afghans with missing legs or mangled hands. Sometimes the mangled hands are from bomb makers who have targeted the coalition, but generally it's from kids trying to make a quick buck by defusing them and selling the scrap for cash. Those with missing legs, just have bad luck in a country with nonexistent medical in-frastructure.

Allegedly Bin Laden has been captured or killed. Everyone is running around and clapping their hands, but I don't see the importance. He wasn't a major factor in this phase of the war. The father-son team of Jalaluddin and Sirajuddin Haqqani is alive and well, and Gulbadeen Hekmatyar and his militant group with Al-Qaeda ties is doing fine. Taliban founder Mullah Omar is allegedly still alive. I can't even begin to list the dozen or so organizations that have sprung up in Pakistan in recent years that regularly target Afghan government officials and Shia Muslims. None of them are household names, as the media have focused on the boogeyman of Osama Bin Laden for years. Of course, in the greater campaign against terror his death might be rele-vant, but in regards to success or failure in Afghanistan, it's irrelevant. Regardless, if Bin Laden is actually dead, I expect there to be some backlash from at least some of the Al-Qaeda fringe groups around the world.

*The amount of UXO in Afghanistan is subject to debate. In the mid-90s, UNI-CEF projected the amount of UXO in Afghanistan at over 10 million (1). However, in 2004, the founder of The Halo Trust, an NGO specializing in the removal of landmines, expressed skepticism at numbers he perceived to be severely inflated. Guy Willoughby estimated that the Soviets placed approximately 250,000 based on records provided by the Soviet-backed government of Mohammad Najibullah Ahmadzai (2). The most frustrating issue for clearing operations is not the well-marked and documented Soviet minefields but the uncounted mines planted by the Najibullah government after the Soviets departed, the Mujahedeen during the civil war, and the Taliban government from 1996 to 2001 as they continued to battle the Northern Alliance. The Halo Trust estimates go as high as 640,000 landmines laid in Afghanistan since 1979 (3). Regardless of the debate on the daunting numbers of mines in Afghanistan, there are over 1,000 casualties each year in Afghanistan according to the independent watch-dog organization, The International Campaign to Ban Landmines (4).

May 3rd

I am frustrated at the lack of patriotism and optimism from the Afghan-Americans with whom I share a tent. It's apparent that none of them give a damn about this place and just want to make some money quickly and go home. I'm also frustrated at the constant complaints about conditions. They are dismal, but at the rate they pay us and the relative luxury compared to the guys in the field, there is little room for the griping. We are some of the highest paid contractors in the country with paychecks of nearly $20,000 per month and the first ~$90,000 tax free if we stay an entire year. It's a tragedy in a sense, when one considers that some of us make more in a month than a private in the Army makes throughout an entire year. It's also a tragedy when one considers that we can leave whenever we like, and a military member is stuck here anywhere from 6-24 months depending on his service and luck. It seems the older Afghan-Americans are the ones who complain the most. Decades of relative wealth in America has made them soft. I enjoy my conversations with the green-card holders who are hungry and enthusiastic. They spent years as local-national linguists and after doing their time, finally earned enough money to get through the American diplomatic hoops for a work visa. They have an odd ambivalence about them in their desire to help their homeland in a manner that may take them from their homeland for good, if their path to US citizenship is complete. War is filled with catch-22.

I went to kill some time at the bazaar; where each day, local businessman shuffle through the gate to set up shop to sell a variety of goods. Unfortunately, I don't have any cash, so I feel like an ass for browsing. The high-quality woodwork is my favorite commodity, with boxes that have secret entries and hidden compartments. The hand-crafted jewelry from various precious and semi-precious stones common to Afghanistan is riveting in its quality. The most interesting items are the leftovers from decades of war, including 100-year-old Enfield rifles.

Even though I was unable to purchase goods, the shopkeepers invited me for tea and sweets, and we had a long discussion about the war and reconciliation in Afghani-stan. I've never had to use both Pashto and Dari simultaneously, so being bombarded with questions from a lone Pashtun and two Tajiks in both languages simultaneously gave me a headache. While they got along, it was amusing to see the Tajiks blame Pashtuns for the war and for the Pashtun to blame everyone else. We also discussed the recent death of Bin Laden, which solicited an immediate and visceral dislike for Arab interlopers. Afghans are often ambivalent about the Taliban for a variety of rea-sons, but no one has anything nice to say about Bin Laden and Al Qaeda.

I've got the bazaar to myself today. Public areas are ghost towns today with everyone edge over potential retaliation for Bin Laden's death. Nothing substantial has happened in the country, but we'll keep waiting.

I experienced my first mortars tonight. An Indirect Fire (IDF) alarm went off before the double "whoomp" of impact somewhere near the airfield. No one was hurt, to my knowledge.

[Letter Home: May: 4th] Kevin, this is a short humorous essay I wrote on transient living. Please enjoy.

I'm still in the transient tent; it's the third day in Afghanistan. The tent contains 100 beds squeezed into approximately 2,000 square feet. In theory, 100 people will be crammed inside the space equivalent to an American home—in theory. In reality, the wave of new arrivals that I came with swelled the tent to 105 people, and the wave that arrived today added an additional 10. I was fortunate on the first day to be faster than some of my older compatriots to snag a bed. Fortunate is a relative term, because it was a top bunk next to the wall of the tent as well as the door. Besides the obvious disturbance of a door opening and closing 24 hours a day, there is the bonus of 100-degree heat radiating off the canvas, which when whipped by the wind, whacks whatever part of the body is adjacent to the edge of the tent. The mattresses have been used and abused by god knows how many thousands of transients filtering off to parts unknown in Afghanistan; they show the wear and tear. One can look past the shards of protruding metal and torn fabric, but one cannot ignore the coils pushing off in random directions as each portion of the body is met with a different level of tension and absorption. The subtle mounds of discomfort in the mattress aren't noticeable at first, but in the middle of the night, as vertebrae pop out of alignment, and the spare tire around my midsection is now pinned between coiled springs jockeying for dominance, it's noticeable. I'm better off than my colleague though. He spent the first two nights on the floor of the makeshift mosque built into the corner of the tent, and he managed to find nearly every rock in Afghanistan. He squirmed in agony for the first night. When there are less people, eight patches of carpet are lined up to face Mecca, and during the five mandatory prayers of the day, there is a near constant filtering in and out to commune with God. As more people trickle in, and beds are no longer vacant, the mosque is reduced in size to seven, then five, and then one, as sleep takes precedence over salvation. The spirit is willing but the flesh is weak?

Halfway through my second day, a friend waved me over to an open bed. After years of military training, I'm primed to move out in a moment's notice. I spring from the Marquis de Sade of mattresses with my sleeping bag in tow, and slalom through the maze of bunk beds to spring upon my deliverance. It was still on a top bunk, but at least I was away from the door, away from the side of the tent, and away from the mosque. Even better, the next morning, I lay in wait as a group of personnel began filtering off into parts unknown in Afghanistan. Before the mattress of the departed has even cooled, I slinked over in my boxers to mark it with my sleeping bag. My prize is a bottom bunk.

I try to take ownership of a place that I plan on calling home for more than a couple nights, and though there is a chance to upgrade to a better bunk closer to the electric outlets in the tent, I'm satisfied with what I have. I sweep out weeks, months, or years of accumulated dust, trash, and mouse shit. Then I dust off the flat surfaces of my bed. Now I'm protected by a wall of relative cleanliness, and hopefully newly arrived dust and debris will find purchase on the railings of my bed and not enter my lungs; I have a cold from sometime around Frankfurt, Germany on a layover. Using my penknife, I drill holes about four inches apart along one edge of the bed, and using an old shredded extension cord, I weave it up to hold a blanket onto the railing of the bunk bed to block out the light on three sides and use a poncho across the fourth. Now I can sleep in complete darkness with a limited amount of soundproofing. Of course this darkness does come with casualty, and in the first night of taking advan-tage of the privacy, I accidentally grabbed a tube of hair gel by mistake when I wanted lotion; war is hell.

On one of my perimeter runs, I spotted a few unused cinder blocks, and plenty of spare wood, so I constructed a bench to sit on while I type, write, or read. More improvements might be forthcoming, but at least for now it's beginning to feel like home.

One more bit of housekeeping is laundry. With no public laundry facilities here, the only option is to drop it off at the laundry depot for it to be washed en masse with a three-day wait for return. I hope I'll be out of here before three days, so I'll be doing a load of laundry in the sink and drying it off on a piece of 550 cord tied to the lines se-curing the tent. At a temperature of well over 100, steady wind of approximately 15 miles per hour, and nearly no humidity in the air, drying clothes on the line takes less time than the conventional clothes dryer; I'm going green.

Waiting for work is a good time to finish up a term paper that is overdue for my MA in International Relations, and write some letters home.

At night the tent has a feel of Boy Scout camp. I don't suppose the Afghans know the words to "John Jacob Jingleheimer Schmidt." Though given that Jan is a popular Afghan name, I think we should be able to meet in the middle on this one. Soon I'll have the whole transient tent singing Jan Ahmad Gulbadeen Karim. It's the best I can do for syllabic and rhythmic matching; I'm no poet.

Steve

May 4th

I'm doing my best to use my time wisely. I'm irked at the idea of wasting so many tax dollars because of inefficiency between my parent company and the military. I've now been here for over a week, and I've cost the US taxpayers $5000 without lift-ing a finger for work. I write letters home, read copious amounts of low-rent fiction, and work on my degree. I'm in the final class, and I'm debating between doing a the-sis and taking the easy way out with the Comprehensive Exam. It's only a bullet point on a resume so I'll probably just go with a Comprehensive Exam. There is a reason-able stigma attached to an online degree, but I think I've gotten my money's worth from American Military University.

The anti-malaria medicine, doxycycline is causing sun sensitivity, and I'm getting burned with only a few minutes of exposure. I think if I switch to taking the pill the night before the greatest effects of the drug will be weaker in the harshest daylight.

[Letter Home: May 5th]

Dear Mom and Dad,

I've called a few times, but no one answers. I'm assuming you're on vacation or in an advanced state of purification. Hopefully the former, as this letter would be pointless otherwise.

Right now I'm a transient resident of Bagram Air Field. I'll eventually be as-signed to Herat which is in the west, adjacent to Iran, but as there isn't much activity there, it takes a while to get a flight. Hitchhiking is strictly forbidden, partially because it would result in kidnapping, and partially because the thumb up to hitch a ride is offensive to Afghans. As guests in the land of the Afghan, we must be constantly sensitive to the cultural mores of the local populace.

The most interesting thing I have seen so far are these strange metallic disks half buried in the mud. The middle area has a depressible circle that moves up and down and makes an electric clicking sound like a light bulb shorting out. No one will tell me what it is, and whenever I show the Afghans, they yell at me and throw rocks at me when I come closer.

Bagram isn't a bad place for running. I'd estimate roughly 15 miles worth of paved surface and another 15 miles worth of gravel and dirt roads. Of course, as most of BAF is located in the remnants of a Russian mine field, straying far from the tread marks left by the most recent humvee is unwise. This means a fair amount of strain placed on the knees while trying to balance on top of two-inch ridges of dried mud left by the tires. Yesterday, I went running on the perimeter. We are right up against the locals here, and a couple of youngsters grazing their goat herd in yonder pasture of un-cleared Russian mines—such a culture shock to see someone haphazardly follow-ing behind a herd of goats. I suppose you just make sure to step wherever the goat stepped, and if they don't disappear in a bleating vapor of sinew, fur, and plasma, you won't either. Some North African security contractors bouncing up in a Humvee to in-form me in broken English that I couldn't be there interrupted my musings on the culture; they said I had to stay on the "rock road." Given that this perimeter road was cov-ered in golf ball to baseball size chunks of gravel, I have to assume that "rock road" meant the pavement I left a mile previously. Ever prudent, I refrained from quibbling over the fact that the gravel meant I was indeed on a "rock road" already. It seemed ill-timed to debate semantics, with a bunch of North Africans waving M-16s at me. Based on their looks, I think they might have been Sudanese; I'm not sure. Ever pru-dent, I refrained from questioning their ethnic lineage. It seemed ill-timed to discuss the matter with a bunch heretofore unidentified North Africans holding the previously mentioned American assault rifles. I returned along the perimeter road wedged be-tween an un-cleared Russian minefield on the left and a single layer cyclone fence topped with concertina wire on the right. I've seen used car lots with better defensive measures than that fence, but I must add that outside the fence was another mile worth of un-cleared Russian minefield, so to mount an attack, the Taliban would need to cross two un-cleared Russian minefields AND a single layer of cyclone fence topped with concertina wire. I sleep soundly knowing it will take at least another 20-years-worth of IEDs used to kill infidel foreign invaders, which have been constructed from the remainder of the un-cleared Russian minefield, before they even arrive to the daunting single layer cyclone fence topped with concertina wire. About the time I got back to the "rock road," a military security forces guy poked his head out of a guard tower.

Dialogue:
"Hey, I'd stay off the perimeter today, we're gonna be attacked in 30 minutes."
"Is that a daily thing, or just this morning?"
"Just this morning."
"Thanks."
"You know that's a minefield right?"
"Yeah it's marked."
"Okay, just making sure."
"The road is safe though right?"
"Uh ... Theoretically ..."
"Thanks."

We weren't attacked. Typical unreliable Afghans, no follow through. That's one of the biggest obstacles in the reconstruction of Afghanistan. They have no sense of discipline. If you are scheduled to mortar the infidel foreign invaders at 0530, then goddammit, you mortar the infidel foreign invaders at 0530!

Another one of the biggest hindrances to progress is the Afghan's inability to grasp indoor plumbing. After shitting in hastily dug holes for 30 years, the concept of sitting on a plastic seat is difficult. It's common to find shoe treads on the seat after the Afghans have waged expert bombing runs to drop turds deftly into the toilet from altitudes as high as three feet. Maybe we are the ones doing things bassackwards. With that kind of accuracy we probably should teach them how to fly A-10s. At least that way when there were civilian casualties, the Americans wouldn't get blamed. There are occasional accidents with the pipes splattered with fecal matter—the casualties of war I suppose. Always open to new ideas, I thought, "When in Rome," and attempted my own aerial bombing; I'll miss that pair of sneakers. There is a team of 200 aid workers from Finland who have travelled around the country to train and develop the Afghan's ability to use indoor plumbing, but they have had mixed results. General Petraeus has not returned emails or phone calls regarding my idea for Afghan

A-10 pilots; I always took him for an open-minded guy, but I guess his public image is deceptive. Booze is strictly forbidden here. I'm sure some is smuggled in, but in general, it's not available. For some odd reason they have Beck's non-alcoholic beer in the chow hall. The seventh circle of hell has reservations.

All in all, things are great. I'll bitch about living conditions in another letter. My wrist hurts from typing, and I need to save my strength. Me and some buddies are gonna go out to an uncleared Russian mine field and throw rocks.

Steve

May 5th

The cold has finally passed and my lungs have cleared up. I have taken to wrapping my face in a headscarf when walking along the main roads.

I've taken to writing down the various nationalities which are here. I'm up to 20. Things have calmed down since Bin Laden was killed. The day of and the day af-ter, they shuttered the PX for a few hours, and until today, they've had 100 percent ID check at all chow halls and other public facilities. I doubt the average Talib* cares one way or another. While both the Taliban and Al Qaeda are fundamentalist Islamic organizations, the similarities stop there. The Taliban merely want to establish a theocracy in Afghanistan, while Al Qaeda wants to unite the Islamic world against the west. If left alone, the Taliban would never go past the Afghan border. Al Qaeda has always been the real threat to the United States; already the media are suggesting we can go home now, because we got Osama Bin Laden.

*Taliban is from the Arabic loan-word of "talib" which means student. Talib is then pluralized with the Persian ending of "an." It is the proper singular form, though it's uncommon to hear it among westerners.

May 6th

I met another minesweeper today. This guy was from Mozambique. It's interesting that the African Republics are sending minesweepers, but I guess it makes sense given the number of mines in those countries and the relative experience they have with removal. He said that when sweeping areas known to have anti-personnel mines, they keep a 25 meter radius between each other, and when sweeping areas known to have anti-tank mines, they keep a 100 meter radius between each other. It's a testament to the sheer danger of the job given that they stay apart to avoid being a collateral casualty from another's faulty step.

There has been no major backlash from Osama's killing. The pundits are calling for a pullout and ignoring the greater issues of regional stability. If Osama has been the target all this time, then we should have nuked Quetta; obviously we are here for something else. The best news about all of this is that asylum was granted to Osama Bin Laden and not Al Qaeda as an organization, and that allows the Taliban to distance themselves from a group with whom they have few ideological similarities. While both are fundamentalist Islamic groups, Al Qaeda wants to establish Islam as the dominant or even the only religion in the world and openly attacks Western targets everywhere, the Taliban merely wants Islamic law in its own country and to be left the hell alone.

[Letter home: May 6th]

Dear Sheryl,

I honestly don't get too lonely over here—every now and then, but rarely. I like being deployed, because everything slows down. I don't like the fast-paced American lifestyle too much anymore. A lifestyle that demands I blow half a week's pay on my shiny new iPhone and another day's pay each month just to keep the data plan going. When I'm stateside, the refrigerator is right there. Getting something to eat takes all of what? 45 seconds? When I was in Qatar, I had to walk 7 minutes to get to the chow hall. Here it is a little closer, but to get online? Yeesh, I have to take a 20-minute bus ride just to get to it. I don't have a cell phone here. I must connect to an operator the old fashioned way, dial a phone card, and then dial my number. To connect with someone in the states takes almost a minute. There's no chatting on my iPhone on the way to work. I can't just watch the morning news. I mean I suppose I could if I tried really hard, but news here means at the bare minimum, going to Google news and reading actual articles. Taking a shower means gathering up my stuff walking 50 yards, taking my clothes off, showering, getting dressed, and walking back to the tent. I could drop off my laundry, but it takes 3 days to get it back. The speedy way is to wash them in the sink and then hang them on the side of the tent. Fortunately it's very dry here, so drying only takes about 45 minutes. The list goes on.

I'm not complaining about this; I enjoy it. All of these times spent doing little menial tasks the old fashioned way give me some time to compose my thoughts—file all the stuff away and organize it in my head. I don't feel like I can ever slow down stateside.

I've got my books and my notepads; I'll be set. I'm buddies with a couple Afghans, but the fact is, I'm in a transient state, and I don't care to get close to anyone when I know I'm leaving. When I start working with my team, I'm sure I'll get close with them.

One mustn't complain too much. After all, we always have our health. Of course the daily dust storms will very quickly wreck any residual health brought to Afghanistan in a matter of days. If you are unaware of the physics of a dust storm, the earth heats under the suns burning rays, and the super-heated air rises to create a vacuum, and a vacuum creates wind. Afghanistan agriculture is slowly being rehabilitated through coalition efforts, but there are still large swathes of open area with no sort of vegetation. A mixture of gray and brown dust is sucked up by the rapidly increasing winds, and very quickly vision is limited to a few yards. If one is out on a run or long walk, life gets complicated fast, given the un-cleared Russian minefields I've addressed in the past. Sometimes one must go out for official business, and this means penetrating the maelstrom, which is as dirty as it sounds I've got my trusty Afghan headscarf, made in Taiwan, and I put it on. The fact that I now qualify as a rag head means that I am met with the suspicious glares of coalition members, but this doesn't bother me terribly, because I'm not breathing particulate into my lungs. I just give the Afghan good luck symbol and go on about my business. The dust storms usually only last a few minutes. The wind doesn't stop, but there's only so much dust to blow, and like Charlie Sheen, the energy is quickly burned out—winning. Imagine a Midwestern super-cell cloudburst that's over by the time you've gotten the clothes off the line. If caught outside without a headscarf, best make it indoors. Of course going back to my cursed tent is out of the frying pan and into the fire. At low humidity, with a stiff wind, 104 degrees is not too brutal, but 100 people make a fair amount of humidity in the confines of a tent, and the only wind available is what you break yourself. Sweat that was instantly vaporized by wind and low humidity now pools on the upper lip, eye-brows, and gender based nooks and crannies. The dry shirt with salt stains is soaked through in a few seconds; it's hot.

The heat does get to a person after a while. It doesn't matter how much water is consumed or how reluctantly the body is rousted from a resting state, there comes a point when the body is just done, and the mind has had it. I'm hungry; the chow hall is open; they have air conditioning there. I know if I can just make the 200-yard walk to the door, I'll be okay. They have sweet iced tea that's not as good as grandma made but drinkable, and the salad bar beckons to me like an oasis. Yes, I know iceberg let-tuce has little to no nutrition, but I'm desperately grasping for solace, and even if the name were lukewarm lettuce, I'd be satisfied. It's blindingly bright outside, so I grab my sunglasses and slink toward the door, but halfway there, I realize I should grab some reading material, because once I hit the AC, I won't want to leave. I traipse back to grab a tattered copy of Gravity's Rainbow, and again work my way back to the door, before realizing I no longer have my sunglasses. I curse under my breath while am-bling back to my bed one more time, frustrated at my own stupidity. I can't find my sunglasses; I can't go outside without my sunglasses. I begin a meticulous search in my rucksack and on the top bunk. I search the rucksack again, because it's the obvi-ous place for them to be, and the true sign of intellect is to doing the same thing and expecting different results. I've got blinders on to any rational alternative but to con-tinue looking for my sunglasses, so I pull out a duffle bag, and when reaching inside, I immediately turn a fingernail backwards on some unidentified piece of equipment. Now I'm hot, pissed off, and bursting into an unintelligible string of profanity in at

least two different languages. With my left hand, I grab the strap of the duffle bag for purchase and begin pummeling the contents with my balled right fist and tearing open a knuckle on the curved corner of a Nalgene bottle. I know real men don't hit duffle bags, but the bitch had it coming.

I found my sunglasses right where I left them... on top of my head; it's hot.

Steve

May 7th

Twice daily, a truck comes to pump out the

"black water" from the tanks of the bathroom trailer. Black water is human excrement, gray water is from the sinks and chow halls, and of course fresh water is fresh water. I wonder if the tanks ever get mixed up.

Sometimes I wonder if the alleged mortars are merely a drill. I was in one of the rec areas, and a guy looked at his phone and said, "We are about to be mortared." We heard a double explosion and then the sirens. How did he know before both the explosions and the sirens? Bizarre.

May 9th

I've finally got word that I'm leaving on a red eye tonight to Herat via Kandahar Air Field (KAF) on a C-130. I've never been on a C-130; from what I've heard it sucks, so here goes nothing.

May 10th

Kandahar stinks. Once upon a time, the sewage pond was a few miles off base, but the constantly expanding installation has engulfed the sewage pond which has wound up in the center of the base. We are pummeled by the stench with every gust of wind. There are talks of filling it in, but like most non-operational planning, execution is years after conception.

Last winter, the pond overflowed from seasonal rains, and a river of shit covered this part of the base. It flowed through the chow hall which had to be shut down for a week. Tomorrow I'll be on another C-130 to Herat.

May 11th

Herat is as beautiful as I expected, but I won't be staying. I'm on Camp Stone for the night, and I'll be headed out on the first chopper to Helmand in the morning. As expected, my Pashto was useless. I'll admit I was terrified at the idea of going to Helmand. It's more hype than anything, but everyone keeps saying how dangerous it is, but the numbers say it's really not.

Camp Stone is named after SFC John T Stone, killed by small-arms fire in 2006. It's a decent facility with a nearby airfield that is run by Spanish and Italian soldiers along with a few American augmentees. The area is not very volatile, and the trip from the airstrip was in small SUVs with a limited amount of armor and bulletproof windows, a far cry from the nearly invincible MRAPs (Mine-Resistant Ambush Protected) I've seen elsewhere.

May 12th

I am near Ghereshk, Helmand on a giant installation called Camp Bastion, from which, many Danish, British, and Italian soldiers operate. While they were once separated by desert, Bastion I, Bastion II, and Bastion III have grown in size and have met in the middle with Camp Leatherneck, one of the largest Marine installations in Afghanistan. Both Bastion and Leatherneck are only a few years old, but the level of development is astounding, including an 8000-foot runway on Bastion. I'll be residing on Camp Calero, named after Major Jeffrey R. Calero. He was killed by an IED in 2007.

I'll be getting my own room soon, but I'm back in a transient tent; the mattresses are amusing in their lack of utility. They are so old and worn out, one would be better off just sleeping on a cot. I have the option of moving into a container-room right now, but as I have the tent to myself, it makes sense to just stay here rather than take on a roommate*. The only downside is the wind starts in the late afternoon and doesn't die down till about 0400. The tent is not tied down properly and there is a con-stant slapping of timber and loose fabric that makes sleep difficult.

I start work tomorrow; I'm nervous and excited; I hope I'm useful.

Bastion means eating at a British chow hall, and I won't even try to be upbeat about this. British food is awful.

*There are three types of primary housing for coalition forces in Afghanistan aside from the temporary tents I've already mentioned. B-huts are plywood, insulation, and metal roofing, and they can be communal living with an open bay or be divided up into rooms for one or two individuals. Shipping containers have been fitted with plywood and electricity and are used by individuals or pairs. Modular container housing is the most efficient for permanent use and consists of rectangular boxes that can be stacked multiple-stories high. They are a step up from the shipping containers for comfort but are also the most expensive.

May 13th

I'm enjoying my work, for the most part. We are over staffed, in my opinion, with four linguists working only 6 hours at a time. Being overstaffed is a common problem in the military where the number of potential seats filled is important. If it's demonstrated that a unit generally only needs two linguists, when a time comes that they need more, it will be very difficult to justify that need. While competing with high demand commodities (linguists, medics, etc.) it's better to hang on to unneces-sary bodies until they are needed. It's a shortsighted policy that inflates the overall defense budget, but bureaucracy is a funny animal. Dave and Jay are on the day shift, and Sayeed and I are on nights. My supervisor, Gunny Mark, has a grudging respect for me, and while he is a curmudgeon, he is enthusiastic and competent in his job, and I will enjoy working with him.

May 15th

I have a neighbor in the tent now; "Sam" which is short for Salim. He's a nice young guy that doesn't seem to understand that I have no interest in watching porn with him. The military often gives American names to the Afghans. Sam equals Salim. Jay equals Jawid. David equals Daoud. Interestingly enough, Daoud is actu-ally the Arabic word for David, and many Western names have an Arabic equivalent in the shared histories of Islam, Christianity, and Judaism. Jabril equals Gabriel; Isa equals Jesus, and Ibrahim equals Abraham.

There was tuna fish on the pizza at the British chow hall—weird guys.

May 18th

I just met a cute Pakistani-British girl named Saraya, who said she'd help me learn Urdu. She's completely vapid. I've never heard anyone complain more about food, heat, and life in general. I suspect she's going to quit soon. She's only been here for three days, and she's already called in sick twice for headaches. She also seems to struggle with the most basic functions of her job at the British PX. Evidently there is a level of expertise required to run a cash register that she fails to grasp. Despite my cri-tiques, there is something to be said for female companionship, and I'll continue to dine with her and hopefully go on some walks with her around base if she is able to adapt to the heat.

May 26th

I finally have my own container; it is glorious.

May 29th

The Taliban has launched the annual "spring offensive" and it seems to be largely a propaganda campaign with little increase in fighting overall. I sus-pect we'll have fewer than 600 total coalition deaths this year—maybe fewer than 500 for hos-tile deaths.

May 30th

I'm shaving the beard;

it's apparent I'm not going outside the wire, and it really doesn't serve a purpose right now; I can always grow another one, and hopefully Mark will cease calling me John Walker Lindh*.

May casualties are up from last year. There were 56 deaths this month and only 51 last year.

*John Walker Lindh was an American who converted to Islam and traveled throughout the Middle East in the late 90s, eventually winding up in Afghanistan as a member of a group funded by Osama Bin Laden, which supported the Taliban in its effort to wrest control from the portion of Afghanistan still controlled by the Northern Alliance. He is little more than a footnote in the overall war, but my beard warranted humorous comparisons and half-hearted commentary that I was going native.

1.   United Nations Children's Fund, Anti-personnel landmines: A scourge on children, UNICEF, New York, 1994, p. 6.

2. Recknagel, Charles, 2004, Afghanistan: Land Mines From Afghan-Soviet War Leave Bitter Legacy, Radio Free Europe-Radio Liberty
http://www.rferl.org/content/article/1051546.html
3. The Halo Trust, 2013, Afghanistan
http://www.halotrust.org/regions/central_asia/afghanistan.aspx
4. ICBL, 2010, Mine Casualties, Explosive Remnants of War (ERW) and Clus-ter Submunition Casualties in 2010
http://www.the-monitor.org/cmm/2011/maps/map_resources/2011_Monitor_Casualties.pdf
http://www.icbl.org/index.php/icbl/Donate-Now

2

JUNE

June 1st

I borrowed a hard drive from one of the guys in the office. Most have a stash of movies and TV shows in addition to a sizable collection of porn. There is a booming trade of hard drives here as each person brings something to beef up his collection. I don't have a hard drive of my own, but I have some room on my computer, for now.

The amount of porn floating around is staggering. I've seen a one-terabyte drive filled to the brim with nothing but porn—more porn than any person could reasonably watch; one must have goals I suppose. In the absence of women, guys do what guys do. The most disgusting thing I've seen was a DVD titled *Bangin' Mommy*, a collection of gang bangs of alleged MILFs. I told the guys in the office that the entire 106 minutes wasn't worth watching.

June 2nd

I feel something of a moral dilemma. My civilian manager has told me that I get preferential treatment, because I'm a "real American" i.e. white, as opposed to Afghan-Americans. I find his ideas to be repugnant; however, the preferential treatment has allowed me to borrow some language material that has made work at the office easier, and if I tell him what he should do with his idiotic ideas, I would lose access to that. It's not going to make him less xenophobic, so there would be no positive result from ratting on him.

It's good to know how he feels though.

On a lighter note, we have a puppy. A cute little black and white critter who is very docile, unless confronted with another puppy named Juma, who arouses a furi-ous and obnoxious bark. No one has settled on a name yet.

[Letter Home: June 3rd]

Parents,

We've had a cold snap for the last couple days, and with temperatures falling be-low 110, I'm a little concerned it could be the onset of the next ice age.

The office has a new pet. One of the SEAL teams brought a few puppies and now it's underneath my feet while I work. One of the other interpreters will probably adopt her.

"Dave," an Americanized nickname for Daoud, likes dogs. He's Hazara, which means a hatred for Pashtuns in general, and Taliban specifically, is bred into him. Like many Afghan immigrants, Islamic customs have become an anathema to him, though sometimes they cling to some of the larger ideals in Islam. Therefore, a Muslim keeping a dog in his room and bringing it to work isn't that bizarre. Having dogs around has a fringe benefit, because the dogs pick up on the typical Afghan disdain for dogs, and they'll give a woof whenever an Afghan is approaching. Most Afghans are fine, but it's nice to have a heads up when they are coming. The local Afghans in our compound are also Hazara, but Dave is an American citizen.

My other coworkers are "Jay" and Sayeed. Sayeed has resisted the Americanization of his name.

Sayeed is agnostic as far as I can tell; having given up Islam about the time Isla-mists started wrecking Afghanistan. He occasionally catches shit from Afghans who wonder why he eats pork.

He is asked by angry Afghans, "why don't you stand with your Muslim brothers?"

"What have my Muslim brothers done for me besides chase me out of my own country? I will stand with my Christian brothers who respect me as an individual."

Jay is your average Muslim; he drinks, smokes, and I assume he eats pork. His response to [questions about his indifference to Islamic Law] is, "I don't give a fuck." Like most people who don't give a fuck, he's fun to be around outside the office, and when in the office trying to accomplish something, he's unreliable.

This is another good location for running. I've put in about 70 miles so far, and I still have a lot of other running to do before I cover everything. Landmines aren't an issue, so that is nice. The dust is worse; there are hardly any birds to speak of.

Steve

June 3rd

My poor laptop can't handle the heat. I set the temperature in the room at 75, but the room rarely ever reaches that during the heat of the day. These Chigo wall units are still pretty amazing. I wonder which is more cost effective, building a house with a wall unit for each bedroom, one in the kitchen, and maybe one other for good measure, or using central air. I can't imagine it serves much purpose to cool the entire house when only a few rooms get used at any given time.

I'll have to get a fan for the laptop. It's old, but I don't want to get a new computer—oh well.

June 4th

I took a "me" night. I had a couple "near beers,"* smoked a cigar, and took two Tylenol PM while watching the sunset. It nearly matches a night back home. Gorgeous.

*Near beer is the derisive term for the non-alcoholic beer.

June 7th

There are a handful of Afghan workers on this camp who are responsible for picking up trash, carpentry, maintenance, and laundry. This morning, I started up a conversation with them while they were in the gym cleaning and exercising. In Dari, we talked about their lives and education, and the most important thing I gathered was their desire to learn English. I'll need to have it approved by my bosses, but I think it will be a useful thing for the Marines to be able to give basic instructions in English and the Afghans to have another skill. It's also something for me to do to feel more productive. Everyone wins.

June 8th

I have tacit permission from the Marines to start teaching as long as it doesn't interfere with my hours. I said that if my productivity goes down, I'll work extra hours to make up the balance, and everyone seems to agree that this is acceptable. There are two concerns at this point. One, I'll be alone in the Afghan barracks where I could be attacked, and two, a few of the junior enlisted guys complain that they'll have to be careful of what they say if the Afghans speak English. I had no counter for the first concern, for the second concern, I pointed out that any operational communication shouldn't be done in the presence of Afghans regardless of their knowledge of English.

June 9th

Today was my first English class. I have four Hazara students. Habibullah is the youngest and most enthusiastic, and he is also the most educated with most of his leesa or high school completed. One of his aspirations is to go to college when he can save enough money. He also knows the English alphabet and can say it aloud. Lee (Ali) is the oldest of the group, and he is very intelligent. By American standards, he would be a master carpenter and regularly constructs various storage units, cabinets, and other wood products for the camp. He speaks English the best of the four, but he has little formal education in Afghanistan and his writing is weak. Starsky and Hutch are two, so nicknamed, Afghans who look like twins though they are not related. Starsky is very quiet and reluctant to speak. Shy by nature, it is apparent he has a quiet intelligence and I know he comprehends what I say despite his reticence. Hutch on the other hand is somewhat lazy, and I think he attends classes due to peer pressure from the other three.

I provided notebooks and pencils from my own personal stash, but they will eventually fill them. I'm going to write a letter home to a few people and request more notebooks and pencils so I have replacements when the time comes.

They have a white board and a few dry-erase markers that are of very poor quality, but I have some dry-erase markers of my own to supplement theirs. The whiteboard is of poor quality and it's difficult to erase. I'll look into purchasing a white board from the PX on Leatherneck.

I have no idea what I'm doing but I'll figure it out as I go. I began the class in broken Dari and discussed their needs as students. I understand Dari, but it is not my strongest language, because I taught myself while maintaining my Pashto and deploying. I know all the words, but my speech is choppy and my grammar is horrible.

Hopefully the extra practice will improve my Dari in addition to teaching them English. Basically, they want to be independent of the need for a translator for the basic tasks. They also want to know the proper way to address their American supervisors. They have been shouting "Hey!" Habibullah is concerned that this is offensive, and complains of withering glares from the Americans. No one has taught them better.

This is easy to remedy, and I tell them that the default greeting is "sir," but if they know the rank of military members, it would be best if they use that rank. I also went over other basic greetings for them to use, including some informal ones as well as formal ones depending on the scenario. I'm keeping the greetings rudimentary for now.

The most important aspect of my lesson was the directive that they must bring questions to class. I don't want to stand in front of them and lecture with no comprehension. By asking questions, they are directing the lesson, and they will retain the information more quickly.

The shower

June 10th

I found an interesting quote from the Afghan Defense Minister, Abdul Wardak:

"Afghans have never seen [Americans] as occupiers, even though this has been the major focus of the enemy's propaganda campaign. Unlike the Russians, who imposed a government with an alien ideology, you enabled us to write a democratic constitution and choose our own government. Unlike the Russians, who destroyed our country, you came to rebuild."

I've picked up some tendonitis after getting too

exuberant on a run while leaping over massive drainage ditches along the runway. It was fun; I guess I'm getting old. I'm frustrated at my own stupidity, but I guess I'll stay off my feet for a couple days. I don't normally take supplements, but the guys in the office have some creatine, which is supposed to lighten the load on the tendons. I'll try running again in a couple days. If I had some Aleve, it would go better.

Class will be every night after dinner. I'll hope for a minimum of 20 minutes, but I'm prepared to stay up to an hour, and I can get a to-go plate for my meal and eat that at work, so I have more time to teach. I won't teach on Fridays, which is the Muslim equivalent of the Sabbath day. It's good for them and me to have a day off.

Tonight we covered the letters A through E and discussed some common vocabulary that they need around the camp while working. They know a lot already simply because of the repetition. They've been told to sweep repeatedly, but they did not know "broom." They knew "door," but they did not understand "close" and "open" or the imperative verbs associated with that. Hutch speaks Pashto, so when I get hung up in Dari, I can speak in Pashto and he can translate from Pashto to Dari. I don't use this tool very often. Firstly, I want to improve my Dari, but secondly, it's hard enough to learn a language without having to go through two levels of translation.

Each letter is written on the board and I drill it repeatedly. I've also written the words of the day on the board, and though I have not taught them some of the letters, I still drill pronunciation, and when they see these letters later, they will already have an idea of how to pronounce some of them.

I also talked with their American supervisor about what he wants. He said my plan of "work English" made sense and thanked me for telling them about how to respectfully address the Americans. Baby steps. If all I do is lube relations between the Americans and Afghans, I'll be successful.

[Letter home: June 11th]

Parents,

Thanks for the letters.

I'm sorry to hear about the drought. It sounds as bad as the drought in the late 90s. Hopefully you get a little rain and those plants with more robust root systems survive. I wonder if night vision goggles (NVGs) would help to eliminate armadillos. I've been pondering putting together a survival pack and some NVGs are on my wish list. Honestly, NVGs are pretty low on that list, but if I'd actually use them for other things, then they might be worth the money.

As far as immediate safety, I can't think of any real threat. Our compound is huge, and the flat geography discourages indirect fire. There has only been one IDF since I've arrived. My only reaction was to roll over in bed and wonder why the Taliban were so inconsiderate; attacks should not occur before 8 a.m.

With the exception of being ground-based instead of airborne, it's the same as my Air Force job—boring, exhausting, and thankless. I rarely, if ever, get feedback on if I'm creating anything that has any effect, positive or negative.

My most rewarding experience is an English class that I've started. All four students are smart and enthusiastic, and they are all improving. One is a bit annoying, because he's reticent even in Pashto/Dari; getting him to speak is difficult. Three of the students only speak Dari which means I've been forced into improving my spoken Dari. The job I'm getting paid for is Pashto, so in general, I have little motivation to improve my Dari. Teaching this class will be great for that. I don't have adequate re-sources, but I'm doing do as well as I can. I'm going to raid the free library and see if I can find some English dictionaries or other material that is useful.

Teaching these classes is one way for me to take ownership of my time, and if I positively affect these four Afghans, then I feel like I've done something important. I hope to someday have an opportunity to teach in Jalalabad or Kabul. Both have good universities, and Jalalabad University even managed to stay open during the Taliban government. There are friends I could stay with in Nangarhar if I can ever pursue that goal. Security is generally good in both places, but it'll have to improve before I'd be willing to teach outside the wire. That kind of job would unlikely be as lucrative as this job, and though it's not about the money, if I'm risking getting my leg blown off, I'd like to be able to make my mortgage payments.

I'm sure my services would be useful stateside, and I could see myself doing something with Teach for America, but in general, I've grown more and more contemptuous of Americans lately. This recession has just exacerbated a certain disdain for a culture that is given practically every tool in the toolbox, but can't do for itself—blaming their problems on every conceivable entity instead of taking the initiative and fixing themselves. I hope this scorn is blunted with time, but I'm not optimistic. It's interesting to watch my students literally scramble to get ready for class, eager for a lesson, which is short or long as my schedule allows. When I juxtapose this enthusiasm with a recent comment from an acquaintance who lamented that the government was "forcing" his children to learn Spanish, I have to ask, is my scorn still unwarranted?

I've been averaging about 20 miles a week since I arrived to Helmand. That usually consists of 2 long runs, 2-3 short runs, and then off days for the remainder of the week dedicated to other exercise or just resting. I'm cutting weight as well. That telecommuting job combined with a lack of discipline really helped me pack on the pounds. My goal is to drop a pound a week for the first six months of the deployment, which means I'll be down below 160. That's a bit extreme, but it's a healthy rate of weight loss; so far, I'm slightly ahead of schedule. When I'm down a little bit lower, I'll start doing speed-work. I've always had a love-hate relationship with speed-work. I love being able to run a 5-minute mile, but I hate doing the work it takes to get there. I've been reluctant to do speed-work at a higher weight just because it's harder on the knees. I should be starting that in the next two weeks, which will make cutting weight even easier, because sprints keep my sluggish metabolism much higher. I need to borrow a vehicle and figure out some distances for speed work. The [odometers] are in kilometers, but that's not much of a problem.

Steve

June 11th

I met a Marine who was recently shot through the calf. The wound was clean and crisp, so he's on light duty for 2 weeks before going back out in the field. These are some of the most awe-inspiring men I've ever met.

I continued alphabet lessons with my students. I think they will retain these lessons, because on my way to the chow hall at lunch, I found Habibullah drilling the other three on the previous lessons. I chuckle to myself when they call to me across the plaza. "Hello sir! Howz it goin'?" They've learned something. I had originally planned on the alphabet taking five days with five letters a day and six on the final day, but they are showing a remarkable ability to pick up such a simple lesson that I think I will press ahead more aggressively. Tonight I pushed forward to L which means I can finish the alphabet in four days.

The Afghans trust me to know what I'm doing, so I'm approaching the lessons with false confidence. English as a second language is a specialty for those with a BA in teaching. I've never taught anything beyond first-aid and knots in Boy Scouts.

Today I told them I was giving them two of the most valuable tools in learning a language.

"What is this?" and "What is that?"

"I have a question," was a phrase taught in the early lessons of both Pashto and college Spanish, but it's largely unhelpful, because the student does not have the background to ask the question or understand the answer. However, by keeping it down to both a basic level of knowledge and instruction, the student can go far with two simple phrases.

June 12th

Hazaras are sometimes referred to as the "Mexicans of Afghanistan." It's not a derisive term and it's hard to not respect an ethnic group that is willing to travel and perform almost any task in an effort to improve their lot in life. All four of my students are from the Jaghori district of Ghazni, which has a large enclave of the Hazara ethnic group. Habibullah says that the people are very well educated and that there are no Taliban in that district. The Hazara have been at the bad end of several waves of ethnic cleansing during the civil war and the Taliban government, but they are not entirely innocent themselves. The oppression has resulted in the Hazara turning inward and building up their own society within the larger Afghan society. While the Taliban were destroying schools, the Hazara have continued to educate their children. This explains how all four of my students know how to read and write in Dari in a country where nearly 60 percent of men are illiterate. The overall literacy rate in Af-ghanistan is 28 percent with a huge divide in rates between men and women—43 per-cent and 13 percent respectively (1).

June 13th

Whenever my students ask me about my culture, it gives me an opportunity to talk to them about their culture. I'm leery of pressing them on inconsistencies and idiosyncrasies, but when they are the catalyst, it gives me an inroad to tactfully query them. Everything I say in English, I parrot in Dari, so they are getting exposure to the language. I'm a student as much as I'm a teacher with this method, because I sometimes have to pause to clarify a word or to back track when I'm not comprehended. My Dari is rapidly improving though.

Tonight I was startled by Hutch's circular logic about the ethnic hatred in Af-ghanistan.

"Hate is wrong; it has destroyed Afghanistan, but the Pashtuns hate us, so I must hate them."

All four of my students have lost someone to the Pashtun dominated Taliban, so it's difficult to criticize them. I simply put forth the statement that Pashtuns feel the same way. Hazaras hate them, so they must hate Hazara's. Habibullah and Lee assented to the logic, while Starsky and Hutch just glared at me. Both of them have lost uncles in the constant fighting.

I've started bringing tea to class with me as an icebreaker. Afghans take their tea seriously, and while the Lipton Green Tea is certainly of low quality compared to what they typically drink, it's a simple method to build trust and mutual understanding.

I've concluded the alphabet and I am moving on to simple present tense. While present progressive is the more common tense in English, there is no progressive tense in Pashto or Dari, so I'm unsure of whether I should focus on progressive or simple tenses. I would rather my student be able to say the simple tense of "I sweep" and add the time indicator of yesterday, today, now, or tomorrow. I know that they will retain these lessons and that they will be understood. It's better to focus on comprehension first, and they can always improve grammar later. I did a simple game of charades with them saying the first-person simple present tense. I mimed sweeping and picked on Habibullah to say, "I sweep." His enthusiasm is infectious, so I start with him and go around the table with Lee, Starsky, and Hutch repeating after Habibullah.

I have also started eating dinner with my students, as a prelude to class. It's an opportunity to discuss things in a different setting. I am a little uncomfortable talking Dari or Pashto in a more public setting, because anyone could hear me, but I can't think of any direct danger posed to me in this location.

June 14th

Today I learned that the Muslim rest day of Friday actually starts on Thursday evening. It's similar to the strict observance of the Sabbath among some Jews, who begin their day of rest on Friday at dusk and conclude it 24 hours later on Saturday at dusk. Since I was already prepared to teach, Lee rousted everyone else from their nap for class and we had a sleepy review of basic words and then simply talked in Dari for a bit about their lives and aspirations. Habibullah is definitely looking to go places in life with plans for college. Lee appears to be in his early 40s, so I think he's happy with his lot in life as a carpenter. Neither Starsky nor Hutch want to be laborers for the rest of their lives, but neither had any sort of plan to speak of.

None of them have any interest in the military.

After a relatively unproductive lesson, we agreed that there is no class tomorrow and that next Thursday, we will have the break at the proper time.

I am thankful for the break. I find teaching to be absolutely exhausting, mainly because of my difficulties with the language. I think I'm tapping into completely unused territory of my mind.

June 15th

Jay is leaving; I'm going to pick up the slack now. I've been a waste of tax dollars working only 6 hours a day, but we were overstaffed with four linguists. Now that his chair will be open in the morning, I'll start working nine hours and increase my time from there. When I asked Mark about how many hours I could do, he shrugged his shoulders and said, "Whatever you want to do man." I want to work; that's why I'm here. There is an older female terp (slang for interpreter) in the compound. Mia, short for Fatima, is attractive despite her 42 years of age. I have a blatant interest in her and she's invited herself to my container for a movie. I usually read signals incorrectly, so I don't expect this to go anywhere. Males and females are explicitly forbidden to be in each other's rooms, but at the ground level, everyone seems to look the other way. Unless someone complains or the lust is so obvious that it negatively affects the working environment, most people look the other way.

June 16th

Class resumed today. I'm continuing to expand on simple present tense. Mia, along with a local-national translator who is travelling with her and her team, came to class with me and helped with the lesson a little bit. It was nice to have the support of two others in the lesson since I still lack confidence in my Dari ability.

June 17th

I was hit with a mild conflict of interest when I had to translate between Hutch and his supervisor. Hutch didn't show up for work, and at 1000, we banged on his door to wake him up and learn that he had a severe headache and had not slept the night before. His supervisor said that he could sleep till 1400 but that he would have to work late in the evening. He was also told that if this happened again he would get fired.

When Hutch came to class, I talked to him about his headaches which I think are probably a nutritional issue. It was a good chance to teach some anatomy and medical terminology, so they learned a new round of words like headache, hand, and foot. I talked to all four of them about drinking water in the evening so they would wake up on time and be more productive. The chat was directed at Hutch, but by talking to all of them simultaneously, I could avoid embarrassing Hutch. I don't know what the Afghan diet is in most of the country, but when I eat with the four, they eat nothing but meat and rice, and I've never seen them have more than a few sips of tea or a bitter fruit drink served in the chow hall. I suspect that Hutch was simply dehydrated.

June 19th

I tried to hook up with Mia for a second night, but she felt uncomfortable and left with no warning; it's too hot anyway.

I'll take a sleeping pill and rack out for the night.

June 20th

Tried to get a student to say, "I like success." The result was, "I like sex." Close enough, I almost fell down laughing, and after explaining what sex was in Dari, they go the joke and laughed with me.

June 21st

I'm moving on to Mirmandab, which is out in the boonies. It's not far from here by a direct route, but to get there safely, we have to take a paved route through the city of Ghereshk which can take up to three hours. Mirmandab is part of a relatively new concept called village stability operations (VSO) which woos villagers away from the Taliban while simultaneously setting up Afghan Local Police (ALP) and helps them develop their local capabilities. Previously there have been two, largely unsuccessful, methods of policing Afghanistan. First, the coalition tried the top-down approach of the Afghan National Police (ANP). Afghanistan does not have a history of strong central government, so the ANP have never had much credibility, especially among Afghans who have reported the policemen to be largely untrustworthy and corrupt. The second attempt was to fund existing militias. There was no realization that the influence of the militia did not extend beyond a very limited range, and that the militias would often attack each other in a continuance of old feuds. The militiamen, called 'arbakian,' have a dark history in the region, so it was no surprise when villagers were resistant to submitting to groups that regularly shook down travelers for quick payday. Mistakes like this have continually given traction to the Taliban, which have long been viewed as an incorruptible force in Afghanistan. It is irrelevant to point out the endless corruption perpetrated at the hands of the Taliban, because they are still perceived positively. Many can tolerate limited freedom, in exchange for security with the Taliban in charge of their villages. VSO uses Village Stability Platforms (VSP) like Mirmandab as a way to improve upon old methods by recruiting ALP members directly from the village to be trained by Special Operations Forces (SOF), which include US Army Special Forces (SF), Navy Seals, and Marine Special Operations Command (MARSOC).

I'm sad to leave my class so quickly after starting. I gave my English to Pashto/Dari dictionary to Habibullah with the request that he try to learn five new words a day. My goal at DLI was to learn 10 new words a day and by the time I graduated, my working vocabulary was well over 3,000 words. I think twenty is far too ambitious for these gentlemen without any formal instruction, but if they can learn five new words a day, they will have a working vocabulary of over 1,000 words by the end of the year. I've read that the average American adult uses only 1,000 words on a regular basis. I don't know if that's true, but if my students have learned the most common 1,000—words I'll be happy.

The last thing I said before leaving the class was to remind them the best tools they had are "What is this?" and "What is that?"

June 22nd

Hurry up and wait... I was told to be ready at 0900. I woke up at 0730, showered, and packed the last of my stuff, before I was told 1200. I unpacked my laptop and got some work done till 1400 when I was still waiting for the knock on my door. I found the guy in charge and found out "1500 but possibly later." At 1700, I put my

stuff on the back of a truck and took a nap. At 2200, I was told 0430. An entire day wasted; I would have gone to work and taught another English class if I had known.

I'm leaving the bulk of my stuff here, because I expect to only be gone for two weeks.

June 23rd

We left at 0900. Our route took us through the city of Ghereshk. I got to see the bustling industry of the area as we passed a long line of vendors selling everything from fresh melons to used cars. The Toyota Corolla is one of the most common vehicles in this country, and vendors have bought them wholesale from the West. As we crossed the Helmand River it was apparent that the river is used for everything from drinking water to a sewer. Children were bathing alongside herds of goats, which were being herded across the relatively shallow waters typical of this time of year. Irrigation pipes extended into the water powered by gas or diesel powered generators that pumped the water to its destination via clay pipes, but alongside the irrigation pipes there were other pipes that appeared to be for discharge into the river.

In several places there were traffic jams, and children hopped on the sides of our MRAPs to try and steal whatever was not tied down. After the third raid, one of the MARSOC guys hopped out and chased a kid down, who ran off screaming. I guess he knew the lay of the land better than I, because I can't imagine hopping out of the truck and running into a crowd of people like that. The army sergeant across from me popped a hatch and stuck out his rifle as a show of force. I popped my hatch as well and got a lot of great pictures as we cruised through town.

I'll write more about Mirmandab tomorrow; I've got to get some rest and prepare for my first day on the job here.

June 24th

Shortly after I woke up, I was warned about a controlled detonation. Someone accidentally threw a grenade in the burn pit, and it had to be disposed of.

There were a bunch of stray cats in a catfight by the latrine this morning. There is a huge, black, German Shepherd named Hugo, who lives near the latrines. Nick, the dog handler, has warned me to stay away from him. Nick, the dog handler, is a raucous fellow with a great sense of humor. However, his friend Nick, the EOD expert, is filled with complete contempt for contractors that he readily sends my way. I don't mind, because in general I agree with his opinions of the way we have allowed so many military jobs to be outsourced to people like me. He is a great source of information and I enjoy listening to his rants about the war, but I'm careful to not openly contradict him, because it results in a very one-sided argument that seems to verge on violence. He's competent in his job, so I don't particularly care if we like each other.

Ali is another Afghan-American, who is only here for the money and regularly comments that he will leave as soon as he hits his six-month mark, which results in a completion payment of $15,000. We aren't allowed to call it a bonus, which is fair, because you get it regardless of your competency. Ali is unaware of the general contempt for his selfishness and doles out copious amounts of advice learned from a life of relatively mundane accomplishments. Asad's reputation of arrogance and uninformed opinions had preceded him at Camp Calero. He's from Brooklyn and behaves like a member of the Jersey Shore cast. Despite all of this, I respect him for taking a leap such as this, and I think he's dedicated to the job. Also, he seems to be competent in the language, and I'm jealous of his ability to go out in the field.

[Letter Home: June 25th]

Dear Claude,

You specifically asked me to describe the climate and geography—I will aim to please.

I'm in Helmand province, which is primarily a desert province in south central Afghanistan. A relatively large river runs through, though in the driest and hottest parts of the year, it can slow to a mere tickle that is easily crossed by children and herds of goats and sheep. The banks are the only testament to the raging torrent that it becomes in the wet months during the winter. The banks tower some 15-20 feet over the riverbed and as typical of deserts unconditioned to rain flow for much of the year; little of the monsoon can easily be absorbed, so the Helmand River fills to maximum capacity.

There have been numerous deaths of coalition troops in past years from drowning after being swept downstream in one of the many tributaries while ambitiously try-ing to cross on foot or in a vehicle. The Taliban will mine bridges, so they are avoided, but during the wet months, damned if you do, damned if you don't. One must risk drowning or exploding to get the job done. It took too long, but the military has finally created a quick release tactical vest that can be shuffled off with the easy pull of a ripcord. This allows approximately 30 pounds of Kevlar and ceramic plates to be removed to increase the likelihood of survival. The most depressing thing is that historically, people drown in pairs. One guy goes in, and a second guy tries to save him. The main river flows mostly north to south in this region, but further south, it makes a jog westward into the desert and dries up.

The river is referred to as the green zone, because immediately adjacent to it is an area teaming with life. It's interesting name coincidence given that in Iraq, the green zone was an arbitrary military designation for the most secure (and highly sought) area in Baghdad where all the foreign embassies and high ranking personnel were kept, while the green zone here in Helmand is the most dangerous area and is still largely held by Taliban. Both the natural ecosystem and irrigated crops survive in the area nearby. Of course, opium is the biggest cash crop and is harvested in late spring, but corn, wheat, and other crops are produced in bulk as secondary crops. The Taliban take a tax against the villagers and that tax is usually paid as a percentage of the opium, which the Taliban can hoard or sell, to use to pay its soldiers and/or buy weapons.

The elevation here is approximately 3000 feet above sea level, but the area is heavily dotted with mountains exceeding 5000 feet. There aren't any well-developed mountain ranges that I can readily observe, but there are small chains here and there that run for a few miles and peter out.

Most of the natural plant life is low scrub with some trees under 50 feet tall. I'd compare it to life along the Rio Grande. It's unremarkable in general, but it carries a fair amount of wildlife. Whenever I'm adventurous (or dumb) enough to go up in a guard tower for a few minutes, I can spot a new bird species. The guard towers directly to our east border a small irrigation canal that attract a large quantity of animals. So far, I've seen around 25 species of birds and a few small mammals including a generic "desert fox."

Steve

June 25th

I miss my pre-fabricated living container now that I am residing in a B-hut, which is approximately 8' X 8' X 8'. I have a wall unit for heating and cooling, and it is effective in all but the hottest part of the afternoon. A fan would remedy that, but I have no access to one.

I visited the Afghan barracks tonight to discuss an English class with the Afghan Special Forces (ANA SF). It appears that most of them speak Dari, but there are a few who only speak Pashto, so I'll be teaching in both languages. My Dari has gotten to an acceptable level now with all the practice.

I can include the Afghan workers as well. So far I've only met "Fingers" who enjoys the moniker for his missing thumb and damaged index finger, which were blown off at the age of 12 while attempting to dismantle a land mine for scrap. And his nephew "Cowboy," who is so named for his proclivity of always wearing a hat.

[Essay on housing in a combat zone]

Having lived in a B-hut for 3 months in the hottest part of a Helmand summer, it amuses me and bothers me to no end how much value Americans place on their homes, how much we've been affected by the mortgage crisis, how our values are completely out of place in this country. The construction is humble; I'll admit that. There

is no insulation to speak of, and the plywood is only one layer thick. I know the numbers I'm going to put up do not reflect the exact amount one would pay to construct a home in America, but it gets us to the general idea. I'm also not a construction expert, so if I leave something out, I apologize to everyone in a hardhat. I don't know your job.

My little B-hut is approximately 24 pieces of plywood, 32 2 X 4s 16 2 X 6s, and 22 corrugated metal panels. At Home Depot, the range from low quality to high quality would be $1,000-$1,800. That's not buying wholesale, that's walking in off the street and paying the ticket price at Home Depot. A group of four guys slapped it up in two hours, max. They wired it. They installed a wall unit air conditioning unit.

How much would construction be for a starter home? By starter home, I don't mean a monstrosity in an upper-middle class neighborhood with a mortgage payment of $2,500. I'm talking about what my parents bought when they first started out— 1,000 square feet with two bedrooms, two baths, a living room, maybe a sewing room/ office, and a kitchen. It didn't have granite counter tops or mahogany. It didn't have central air and heating, but it did have a wall units. Ceiling fans were a luxury.

Using the high-end price of the materials in my B-hut, it cost ~$30 per square foot, so 1,000 square feet should be ~$30,000. I'll overestimate on new plumbing and wiring and say its $10,000 each. I'm up to ~$50,000 now. I know there is more; I know I need ceiling fans and some wall units in the bedroom; I know I should get a hood for the oven, and I'll need to shell out some money for bathroom fixtures, but the average home price in the US is nearly $250,000. I've spent $40,000 on my imaginary home for the basic structure, wiring, and plumbing, but where does the other $210,000 go?

The American dream should be elevating ourselves to another level, but one that has to be sustainable. Our "keeping up with the Joneses" economy and lifestyle is eating itself from the inside out. It shouldn't take a guy in a plywood shack to point that out, but no one seems to get it.

June 27th

A handful of Congressmen came through today: Duncan Hunter—CA-52, Jim McGovern—MA-3, and Allen West—FL-22.

Congressman Hunter, an ex-Marine, made a lot of intelligent comments and asked numerous valid questions about the VSO/VSP program as well as other ongoing operations. Congressman West made repeated asinine comments that brought about a lot of awkward looks, even from hardened Marines, including that repatriated Tali-ban could not be trusted until they had executed another Talib. The Taliban have the same policy regarding government forces—so do Los Angeles gangs. Congressman McGovern sat quietly. He clarified a few points, but for the most part he took copious notes.

There are some US Army augmentees here for additional security. This allows the MARSOC operators to do the counter insurgency operations without having to constantly watch their backs. Their supervisor is interested in his soldiers learning Pashto, so I'll also be teaching a class of introductory Pashto to some soldiers every other night.

I'm less enthusiastic, because it's obvious that most of them do not want to par-ticipate, but I'll give my best.

[Letter Home: June 28th]

Parents,

A handful of Congressmen are rolling through our area. The whole camp spent the morning scrambling around to make sure the war looked "presentable." The MAR-SOC operators are too busy winning to worry about hospital corners, haircuts, and shaving, so it's an attitude adjustment for them to worry about crap like this. The out-house, which has been slightly askew, was picked up and rotated 45 degrees counter-clockwise. Now we can shit facing Mecca. The pornography, haphazardly tossed around the conference room is neatly stacked and tucked away in a place that's off lim-its to our dear leaders. "Britain's Biggest" might offend their delicate sensitivities. This type of dog and pony show always occurs when someone important comes by. We have to dust off the desert.

Both in and out of the service, I've always found it frustrating. This is how [the troops] live. If you don't like it, go back to the US. It smells bad, because we have to burn our own shit. It's dirty, because we have dust storms. If you don't like it, send more money or recall the troops. I've also found it dishonest that most military com-manders have an attitude of "when the cat's away the mice will play." It's perfectly fine to be lax until someone's boss is on their way. I find the whole ordeal to be dishon-est.

I'll get off my soapbox now.

Referring back to the outhouse, it's not the typical pit dug latrine you might think of. It's a box with a toilet seat in it, and below the seat is an ammo crate. Outside is a container with sealed packages called "wag bags." Each package contains a silver zip lock bag and inside each zip lock bag is a trash bag with its bottom glued into the seam of the zip lock bag. Inside the trash bag is a small amount of white sandy desiccant that tastes like burning. The garbage bag/zip lock bag combo slips through the toilet seat and into the ammo crate which supports the side of the zip lock bag. The mouth of the garbage bag stretches around the toilet seat to make a relatively water/air tight seal. Hopefully you get the idea. Disposal of your sealed zip lock bag is a 200-meter westerly walk to the burn pit. This provides an opportunity for a game I like to call "Bag O' Excrement Toss." Admittedly the name does not roll off the tongue, but I've yet to come up with a better one. It requires an underhanded toss of the zip lock bag into the burn pit. My best distance so far is ~30 meters, but that was with a strong wind. It's ripping good fun, and I'm awaiting word from the [International Olympic Committee] on whether it is considered a winter or summer sport.

Piss tubes

Urine disappears into metal tubes in the ground. I have no idea where the tubes go to, but my best guess is an underground piss lake named New New Orleans.

Steve

June 28th

I was invited to the range today to observe some ALP trainees practicing on the AK-47. I have to say these guys are not bad shots. They shoot a little low, but a gut shot will do the trick as well as a chest shot.

I fired an AK-47 today for the first time. I fired 8 shots with 6 on center mass and 2 on the target from a magazine of 15 rounds. No class tonight with it being Friday Eve (Thursday Night).

It's interesting how much can be crammed into such a small space. The kala or compound is the standard

method of construction in Afghanistan, where walls can be easily built using adobe. Walls are anywhere from 6-10 feet tall depending on the desires of the landowner. Poorer families will usually have a one-room hut in the middle of the compound surrounded by various crops. Richer families will have multiple structures in place and sometimes several families and multiple generations will live in the same compound. We are renting a very large compound from a wealthy landowner; the main wall surrounds three large adobe buildings and a lot of open space. The range in the northeastern most corner, has multiple uses as a helicopter pad, a driving route for ANA SF driving practice, and an athletic field for soccer, football, or any other pastime depending on the players. To the east of the Range are three sets of adobe buildings. One houses the US Army augmentees, the second, next door to the US Army houses the ANA SF, and the third is largely vacant used for storage. There is a second open field in the northeast corner which has a row of containers for the United Arab Emirates Special Forces detachment. Their government has provided them with hot showers and laundry facilities, in addition to a community room with satellite television, and satellite TV in every room.

There are two more adobe buildings in the southeast corner of the facility which provide a residence for the US Marines, the Afghan workers, and the local-national in-terpreters. This area has been supplemented with 15-20 B-huts that provide additional housing. Most of them have been vacated as the Americans have fitted the adobe with reinforcement and plywood to make it more comfortable. My room is one of twelve B-huts in two rows of which six stand vacant. The B-huts are more vulnerable to IDF than the adobe, but as there has been little IDF here, I don't worry much. Also in this area is the American chow hall, and while the ANA SF have their own chow hall, they typically share with us. We also have a shower facility consisting of a gravity drip from a 500 gallon water drum propped up on top of a few HESCO barrier, a pre-fabricated walls designed by the Hercules Engineering Solutions Consortium (HESCO).

To top it off, there is an area set aside for weights, some wrestling mats, stationary bike, and an elliptical machine. There is a treadmill, but for now, there is insufficient power to support it.

The southwest corner and the central area of the compound provides for a burn pit, a supply dump, and a guard tower that stands out above everything else. There are half a dozen other towers that stand vacant but will be ready for use in an emer-gency, and the original adobe walls have been supplemented by HESCO barriers, made of a collapsible galvanized steel cage lined with a synthetic cloth, they can be set up in a matter of minutes to any girth and any height and filled with sand for a nearly impenetrable blast wall. Outside all of this, the area has been lined with razor wire or concertina wire as a final layer of defense.

June 29th

A Navy Chaplain visited the base. He'll be here for about 24 hours and then move on down the line. It's really interesting how they have "combat chaplains" [my term, not official] who are responsible for the salvation and spiritual guidance for guys in a combat zone. He gave communion, but I don't know his specific denomination if he has one.

I went to church, simply because it was something to do. It was interesting to see who came and who didn't. I'm surprised at the number of ardent atheists in the Marines.

I asked students to describe their t-shirt. The result was a student saying, "My shit is brown." Close enough.

I teach class in the chow hall after most everyone has already eaten. It's a plywood shack that gets unbearably hot during the day due to improper ventilation. There are no vents in the roof to allow the hot air to escape, and it's largely airtight, so the heat just gets worse until finally the doors are cracked to allow some circulation. After sun down, the building does begin to cool off and dinner is usually bearable inside. There are a couple picnic tables outside for overflow spots when they run out of room.

There is a small 2' X 3' whiteboard in the chow hall. I've gotten into a good system of writing the English word, the Dari word, and the Pashto word going from left to right across the white board, and then when I get to the bottom of the board, I begin erasing the top few words to make room for more.

June 30th

The Taliban had another largely unsuccessful attack in Kabul, which was quickly repelled by Afghan military and police forces. Ten civilians were killed, six Taliban were killed, and as of yet, no military or policemen have been reported dead. Of course this will be touted as yet another Tet Offensive while it was thoroughly and im-mediately crushed by the competent Afghan forces.

June saw a spike in deaths that went well into the 60s.

1.   2012 CIA World Factbook: Afghanistan People: Literacy Rates

3

JULY

July 1st

There was a shura or council today consisting of some of the local village elders, the local ALP commander, and whatever local men cared to show up. They are patted down before entering the facility as a voluntary security measure. Depending on the type of situation, biometrics data is also collected including a mug shot, finger printing, and genealogical information. Some of the people that show up are Taliban, but the shura is a safe zone, and to my knowledge no one gets detained at these sorts of events. The pat down reduces the likelihood of a suicide vest. Most of the people that show up are just bored younger males with nothing better to do, so the meeting has often already started before all the locals get through security. The shura takes place every Sunday as a way to continue the rapport-building process with the locals and a way for them to air grievances in a way that doesn't make them a target. There is something of an open door policy here, but with Taliban sympathizers observing the facility, it is unrealistic to expect someone to come with a problem during the workweek. There is no food provided, but an ample supply of beverages is available including energy drinks, which are a favorite of the locals.

I didn't do much beyond stand around and observe what was going on and did my best to keep my mouth shut. It was a good chance to observe the local male population. The youngest was a toddler who couldn't even open a juice box on his own and the oldest could barely stand without assistance. The interesting thing was to see them shove a handful of dirt down the front of their pants after urinating. I believe this could possibly be the dry ablution described in the Koran, which states that before prayer, if no water is available, the face and hands should be wiped over with clean dirt (1). This is only an assumption based on the fact that it was close to the noon prayer. It is certainly not the first time that Afghans have had a bizarre interpretation applied to Koranic verse. I could be mistaken, but I have no other theory at this time.

I was outside the shura, but I could hear shouting from inside and asked what was going on, and I was told that the ALP commander gets a little hyper after his third Rip It, an energy drink popular in deployed locations. The typical size of a Rip It is 8oz which contains 100mg of caffeine, vitamins, and an undetermined quantity of guarana.

July 2nd

I met SGT Alba, a humorous and inquisitive guy who loves to talk about a variety of things. He's an Independent Duty Corpsman attached to the Marine units, which means he's gone through some difficult training in Camp Pendleton to get to where he is today, and I've got a lot of respect for him for that reason alone. Aside from acquiring advanced knowledge of battle trauma, he had to run up and down the hills north of San Diego for hours on end with a rucksack. Second maybe to the SEALs, these combat corpsmen have got to be the toughest bastards in the United States Navy. The other guys try to lie and say he's related to Jessica Alba, and to the foolishly gullible, like me, he'll go along with the lie for a moment until he chuckles and says, "nah man, I'm just playin." I'm hoping to exchange some literature with him, because he's complained of nothing to read and I have my own private library I've been hauling around since Bagram. In addition to Alba, there is an army medic named PFC Butz and another corpsman, Billy. Butz is brand new to this stuff, and the convoy to here from Camp Bastion was his very first time on a combat convoy. He's deployed with the 1/505 of the 82nd Airborne, and is a bright young kid quizzed constantly by Billy on techniques that are better in a combat situation and far more advanced than the limited lessons he received in basic medic training. At a glance, most of the guys that came with Butz are on their first deployment save a handful of NCOs. At this time, Butz's biggest aspiration is to get his Combat Medical Badge (CMB), which in a nutshell, means he must provide medical treatment to a unit under fire. Billy is tough to get to know and very dark. He seems like a decent enough guy, and when he hasn't passed out on a hospital bed from exhaustion, he's usually helping with some other ancillary project around the camp. I wish they'd ask/let me help with stuff. It would be a good learning experience and a chance to build rapport. There are strict limitations on the types of duties contractors are allowed to perform, but as lax as everything is out here, I'd hoped they'd ignore that stuff—oh well.

In my English class we covered prepositions. Prepositions are easy to learn when coming from Pashto to English. In Pashto there is a preposition and postposition, so it is less complicated to learn only one word in English, but not everything is so easy. Grammatically, neither Pashto nor Dari has the articles a, an, and the, so understanding when to use them is difficult. We take much of our language for granted, but when considering that names of people, plurals, and group nouns don't need "the" in front of them, it can be difficult to explain why.

Nearly everything about English is irregular.

Grammatically, we can't say, "apple is delicious." It's a fragment. However, we can use a group noun like water in the same sentence and it makes sense. "Water is delicious." is a complete sentence. Additionally, we can put "the" at the beginning of the previous sentence, and it will still be grammatically correct. "The water is delicious."

We can say, "Johnson is going into the room," or "Supervisor Johnson is going into the room," but if we have only a generic person holding a title, we will need to again amend the sentence with "the." "The supervisor is going into the room."

Having studied Spanish, Pashto, Dari, and other languages, I've always been dimly aware of the peculiarities in English, but until studying the language in order to teach others, I have not realized how difficult it is to learn it as a second language or teach it to others.

These students try very hard and it's pleasing to work with them.

There are three local-national interpreters that drop in on class and sit quietly. They are just improving their English passively at this point, and all but one of them is more than capable.

July 3rd

My introductory Pashto lessons for the Americans are still going on, and tonight they interacted with some of my English students, so it was nice to see that. I'm not holding any high hopes for the Americans. I'd hoped to get a select group of interested soldiers, but instead of handpicking the best students, I've gotten whoever hasn't been tasked with additional duties or a guard shift. That's left me with a rotating student body and no sense of continuity between classes wherein I don't know how far along each individual student is.

I went over to the Afghan National Army (ANA) section of the compound today to play chess with Wahid, the Afghan medic who is also one of my best students. He actually took a course in English in Kabul. I beat him soundly in the first game, lost by a hair in the second, and I was ahead by three pieces when he was called up for a patrol and rushed out of the barracks. In the back of my mind, I'm still uncomfortable when I go over to the Afghan compound. Afghan men have such a reputation for sodomy, and I don't want to be a participant, willing or unwillingly.

[Essay on Sex in Afghanistan]

I can't count the number of stories and warnings I've heard from coalition forces regarding homosexuality, bestiality, or "bacha bazi" [child game]. Some argue that Afghanistan remains locked in anachronism—a warrior society where women are for breeding, and men are for pleasure, but I don't believe this is the case. Yes, many Afghans may subscribe to a warrior ethos, and like the ancient Greeks, they may engage in some sort of bonding that includes sexual gratification, but a warrior culture doesn't explain the bestiality or bacha bazi. The cause for these things is something far less innocent.

I haven't seen outright sodomy between two men; I have seen several on the same bed in various stages of nudity cuddling together with wanton looks in their eyes. I am aware of a typically American squeamishness about personal space, but I've been nut-to-butt on third world city buses and thought nothing of it; this was more than just a cultural divide. Coworkers have told me about waking up in the mid-dle of the night in a crowded tent and hearing the sounds of kissing, and I've often seen grown men holding hands while walking together. An SF medic told me about the one Afghan who, when asking questions about how to conceive, was aghast at the fact that he would have to stick himself inside the unclean nether regions of a Pashtun woman. A similar story in Kandahar was of the man who had been regularly beating his wife, because after two years of intercourse, she hadn't conceived. A foreign medic examined her and found no reason she couldn't conceive, and then he remarked that the girl was still a virgin; he'd failed to consummate his marriage in the proper orifice. During the Soviet occupation, small numbers of Russians were unfortunate enough to be captured by the Mujahedeen. The lucky Russians were the ones who just got their throats slit or their heads bashed in, but a select few were kept as war trophies to be raped until their Mujahedeen captors grew bored and killed them.

I have seen infrared camera feeds of Afghans getting it on with livestock. At first glance, I think my eyes must be playing tricks or that I am just ignorant on the intricacies of animal husbandry. Then with exponentially increasing horror on my face and everyone else's, we watched as the guy flipped the uncooperative burro into the missionary position and nearly get knocked unconscious by the flailing hooves. The stories and videos are diverse only in the number of animals that have been abused, up to and including a cow that was too tall for the 60 inch Afghan who needed a stool to commit the act. I don't try to make a habit of watching Afghan bestiality porn. There is no audio, and these guys are far from skilled lovers, but if it's there, it's like watching a train crash into a school bus; I don't want to watch, but I can't look away.

A common term in Afghanistan is "bacha bazi" which translates to "boy play." It's a misleading term, because the participants are generally not small children, but teenagers who haven't developed facial hair yet. They are dressed up in girls' clothing and made to dance to the Afghan equivalent of hip-hop consisting of nothing more than a haphazardly beaten drum with no coherent rhythm. Wealthier older men stand around and watch the dance, and it is common that the boy is sold off to the highest bidder for sexual pleasure. When the boy is old enough to begin growing facial hair, he's released back into the wild. I've known American soldiers who were asked by elders if they'd like to have a dancing boy for the evening, and they've politely declined, but from the perspective of the elder, it would have been a great honor. When asked about bacha bazi, Pashtuns say that it is a disgusting habit and it is something only the Tajiks in the north do. However, when Tajiks are asked the same question, they insist with disdain that it's something only the Pashtuns in the south do. The number of stories from all sides leaves me with no other option but to assume that it is tacitly tolerated throughout the country, and while they might know it's wrong, they lack the resources to combat it, and there are so many larger problems in Afghanistan beyond the deflowering of 13-year-olds.

Some of the homosexuality or the rape of unfortunate Soviet soldiers might be explained away with the warrior culture argument. Military men have always had bizarre bonding rituals from simple hazing to actual sex acts, and until relatively recent history in modern warfare, prisoners were trophies. They might be sold into slavery, executed, and yes, used as sex slaves. The bestiality or spousal abuse might be explained away through commentary on poverty and ignorance. At some point, most Americans have heard jokes told about rural areas in America engaging in such behavior. "South Dakota, where the men run wild and the sheep run scared." However, I can find no apologist argument on behalf of bacha bazi, and while either of the other two can be explained away, when all three are found in one place, I can posit one possible solution. Afghanistan is both an extremely conservative religious society and an incredibly illiterate society. This lends the people to incredibly warped interpretations of the Koran.

In the poorer areas, there is a strict division of the sexes. Women are covered from head to toe when they go outside, girls and boys are schooled separately, and women rarely go to the mosque. Unless the boy is in a position to have an arranged marriage, it is likely he will reach adulthood having never seen a woman other than his mother and sisters. While girls remain a completely foreign concept, the boys have the same physical urges that anyone has, yet they have no method whatsoever of finding release as nature intended. Additionally, I've heard Afghans assert that women are unclean. They don't caveat the statement with "at a certain time of the month" or "before prayer." The statement is absolute. Women are viewed as dirty.

There are numerous verses or sections of verses in the Koran, which when taken in an isolated form, would lead us to believe that women are unclean. See an excerpt from Surah 5:6.

"If you have contact with women, and you cannot find water, you shall observe the dry ablution by touching clean dry soil, then rubbing your faces and hands. GOD does not wish to make the religion difficult for you; He wishes to cleanse you and to perfect His blessing upon you, that you may be appreciative."

When isolated in this format, it would seem that women are unclean, and mere contact with them would require purification, but when taken in context with the rest of the chapter and the time of history in which it was written, it is clear that it refers to sexual contact during a specific time of prayer, something similar to Leviticus 15:18.

"After having sex, both the man and the woman must take a bath, but they still remain unclean until evening."

As is common in cultures with extremely low rates of literacy, many religious beliefs are passed on incorrectly by clerics who are equally illiterate. Verses meant to be interpreted very specifically are interpreted broadly, and conversely, broad generalizations are often narrowed down and taken out of context. In the case of Afghan sexual mores, it is the former. Of course, a response would be, "isn't bestiality, pedophilia, and homosexuality equally condemned alongside fornication?" Yes, it is, but we have the benefit of literacy and a 30-second Google search to prove our points, a luxury that is nigh impossible in most of Afghanistan, and while I don't want to get into a debate on the sliding scale of "sin," given the ever watchful eye of male relatives, it's far easier to engage in illicit acts with other men, animals, or minors than it is to steal away in the middle of the night with a paramour. In the most conservative areas of America, such behavior would result a shotgun wedding or a short jail sentence; in Afghanistan, it would mean summary execution of both the male and female.

None of the above is a statement on morality or lack thereof in Afghanistan society. I'm just observing. Morality is always relative to the culture in which it is being applied, and Afghanistan is far from "normal." I do know in the more urban areas, the country is less extreme. In the secure area that surrounds the colleges and universities of Kabul, men and women in their late teens and twenties can be seen conversing with each other. While not ideal, there are also prostitutes to be found in Kabul. More liberal families will actually allow their teens to date. It is a completely different world from the starkly conservative rural areas which dominate much of the landscape of Afghanistan.

In closing, I'm reminded of the speech at Columbia University by Iranian President Mahmoud Ahmadinejad. There was much dissent over his comments that "in Iran we don't have homosexuals." This was a bad translation. The emphasis was that in Iran (and in the region) there are no homosexuals in a manner similar to the US. They have homosexuals, but it's a badly kept secret; there are no pride parades, lesbian bookstores or men with manicured nails and leave-in conditioner. Homosexuals abound. As in Afghanistan, hormones can only be pent up for so long. It's like this across the ultra-conservative countries of North Africa, the Middle East, and Central Asia. It's not something that's discussed, and if you bring it up, Muslims will always blame it on another ethnic group or another country, but as long as extreme conserva-tive clerics are in charge, it will exist throughout the Islamic world.

July 4th

A British soldier has been kidnapped and likely executed after wandering off base.

Coalition deaths for the month of June were down by 35 from last year's count of 88. A total of 53 deaths; 47 were due to hostile action.

Ramadan is about a month away, and I'm planning on fasting. I'll need to check sunset and sunrise times. Of course it's not as if there is a shortage of Muslims to guide me through it.

There was no 4th of July celebration to speak of beyond a couple of flares which may or may not have been in response to a probe.

[Letter Home: July 5th]

July 5th

Asad saw his first dead body tonight. A member of the ALP was killed in a firefight; the Marines went to his house to give condolences to his wife. Asad continually asserts how tough he is, but he's still quivering hours after the incident. It's amusing, in a sadistic sort of way.

The policeman was named Kadir. Most Afghan names translate to something, and his name means "almighty," in the sense of an almighty God, who was apparently busy elsewhere when Kadir was killed—all part of the plan I suppose. The bullet entered just behind his right temple and exited on the opposite side. One would have expected a more explosive effusion of blood as the body instinctively rushed blood to the

injury, but one of his comrades tried to stop the bleeding with a blanket and it allowed the blood to neatly pool in a small circle less than a foot wide next to the body; Kadir died instantly.

Asad, an American citizen born in Pakistan was the interpreter on the mission, and he had never before experienced death firsthand. For a moment, I felt sorry for Asad, but I really had nothing to say beyond, "that sucks," and I went on about my day. He was in no way responsible for the death; he wasn't even there until after it happened, but he still felt guilty. The fact that he helped in the delivery of the body the family probably didn't help. The young wife and child were both wailing and screaming. Everyone grieves in his or her own way at the loss of a loved one, but I've never heard anyone wail longer and harder than a Muslim woman. It's interesting that on the exterior Muslims appear to be fatalistic; "Insha'Allah" (God willing) is muttered for the most mundane of daily events. The fatalism instantly disappears for death or injury. I feel overly cynical, but I scoff at the idea that God will get directly involved in a person's punctuality, but the person takes death so personally when God let's their loved ones be murdered. One day I'll understand... Insha'Allah.

I didn't know what to say to Asad. He's like most urban males under 30 that I've met—arrogant, brash, and full of himself while having little life experience beyond "clubbing." I suppose humility comes with life experience; most of the city dwellers I've met in the US don't have much life experience beyond clothes and girls. An Airman in basic training spent four weeks bragging about having been in a Chicago gang before being kicked off the firing range because he was so terrified of the M-16 that he couldn't control his shaking or the direction of the muzzle.

Asad is still visibly shaken, but no one really wants to listen; they've all seen more than their fair share of pain and suffering

Alba, the medic simply said, "That's why you get paid so well."

The indifference and apparent callousness of the medic just exacerbated Asad's difficulties in dealing with death, and he lashed out at the medic, "FUCK YOU!"

Alba backtracked just enough to make a point: "Don't take it personal. I mean, we all get paid to do this job. Sometimes we get paid to deal with death."

When Dog handler Nick wanted to know if it was too soon to joke about the inci-dent, Asad gave up on finding some outlet for his frustration and stomped out of the chow hall without finishing his sandwich.

Nick continued laughing.

"I don't want anyone to cry over my death. If any of you come to my funeral, you should joke about it, because that's how I would want it to be. I even got a picture picked out just in case I die!"

He demonstrated what it would look like with his tongue lolling out and two mid-dle fingers raised in defiance.

"You gotta be prepared!"

The morbid chatter continued among those who stayed in the chow hall. July 6th

This morning, Asad seemed to be over it. Everything was spoken of in the past tense, which indicated he was coping with it.

"Man, that really fucked with my head last night; my whole life just played in front of me."

I still had nothing to say; Asad had scrambled eggs for breakfast.

I'm pulling Asad Ali out of class and creating a literacy class with help from his brother. I've overestimated his ability to comprehend, and truthfully, I feel he hasn't been 100 percent honest with me on his capabilities. He comes to class and appears to be writing what I put on the white board, but he is unable to read things out loud on command and his writing in both Dari and English is indecipherable. He is function-ally illiterate.

[Letter Home: July 7th]

Parents,

Sadly, "Bag O' Excrement Toss" is no more. A late release, combined with high winds resulted in a toss falling short of the burn pit. I'll spare you the gory details. I guess I just don't have the discipline for the world of extreme sports.

I'm curious what you think of the growing pool of possible Republican nominees for the 2012 presidential election. I find it dismally lacking. I was optimistic about Bachmann. From the beginning, I disagreed with most of her policies, but I recog-nized a level of personal integrity that I could respect. Regardless of her integrity, her stupidity and/or ignorance is disturbing. She recently signed some silly pledge to pro-tect American families. Among other things, the pledge referenced protecting us from "Sharia Islam." There is no such thing. How can one get so high in politics and remain so ignorant? I have to say Bachmann is just another autocrat clothed in "conserva-tive" rhetoric. She's all about small government unless it's an issue she thinks is im-portant, then government can't get there fast enough.

I'd vote for Ron Paul, but his isolationist rhetoric is a bit excessive as is his talk about the gold standard. I'm not as educated on the subject of gold standard and on the history of the Federal Reserve as I should be, but knowledge of history makes me believe that a gold standard is irrelevant. Hard currency didn't stop the rolling depressions of the late 1800s or the Great Depression. Also, hard currency is from the days of colonialism/imperialism. All one had to do for more currency was to raid some third-world backwater. I don't think we have that luxury anymore. Herman Cain is more of the same, but while Ron Paul can argue his case eloquently, Cain comes off as a blithering idiot. It would be interesting to see him in the election though. A growing number of blacks are voting Republican, because they perceive the Republicans to be the morality party, and a rapidly growing black middle class will also bring more and more recruits to the GOP.

I think Romney is the only candidate who can beat Obama, but in the process of pandering to the nut jobs, he's contradicting many of his more liberal or centrist atti-tudes. As with McCain in 2008, the Romney we see now won't exist in 2012.

The rest of the announced candidates? Well, whether it is fair or not, I think the 2008 election shows that Americans have grown tired of angry white males in the White House, and whether or not they have good ideas, no one is going to vote for

them. The fact that every one of them talks a good talk that doesn't match their actions is beside the point.

I'd see Romney taking the primary and losing to Obama with either Bachman or Cain as his running mate. However, I haven't considered what happens if someone like Palin jumps in. She's already tried to torpedo Romney twice, and she's not even in the race.

Steve

[Letter Home: July 7th]

Allen,

Mirmandab is in Helmand on the east side of the river. It's a "hearts and minds" operation dealing with some ANA SF, ALP, and as much local interaction as possible. My actual official duties are boring and not terribly fun, but every now and then I get involved with something mildly interesting. This morning a couple of kids showed up wanting to see the "doctor," a Navy Corpsman. I translated for that. Most of the work done directly with locals is done by natives. For the most part, I'm too valuable to risk having my head blown off.

I'm teaching on the side for fun, and I enjoy it. I'm teaching an English class to some soldiers and a handful of workers. Depending on the students, I teach it in Pashto and or Dari because a couple of the soldiers only speak Dari. Thankfully, all but one of them knows how to read and write in Pashto or Dari, which makes my job easier. The one who doesn't know how to read or write also wants to learn English and doesn't understand that he needs to learn how to read and write in his own language before he learns English. I have to do extra lessons with him outside of class where we go over words and sounds repeatedly. I'm also teaching a rudimentary Pashto class to some US Army infantry. Unfortunately their supervisor doesn't understand the operative word "voluntary," so I ended up with a bunch of unenthusiastic guys weighing down the class for the handful that are actually interested. I've talked with all of them and found that two of them actually want to be there, so I'm going to adjust class times accordingly.

I should be settled in here for the most part now, but I'm always at the whims of operations, so if I get shipped out with a day's notice—so be it. Operations are going to be shifting more to the eastern side of the country, but I don't know if that's going to affect us or not. It'll be interesting to see what happens over the next one-and-a-half years as we lose 30,000 troops. I would have liked the troop drawdown to be about 20,000, but I imagine a lot of those going home are superfluous staff and sup-port. I'm not exactly sure what a general does, but you can't walk around Bagram for five minutes without running into one. I'm sure we can all do with less "leaders" and more leadership. The ANA are getting more and more competent, and the Taliban in general are more reluctant to hit fellow Afghans rather than the infidel foreign invaders (sarcasm). It'll probably be a good step toward stability to turn over some of the more peaceful areas to local control. More important than the ANA is the ALP. Twenty minutes on Wikipedia would have told our fearless leaders that Afghanistan doesn't have a history of strong central government and that the major power brokers are usually at the district level. It's too bad that it's taken years of bad policy to realize that, but better late than never. The ALP is generally well respected by the locals, because in theory they ARE the locals.

The facilities aren't bad. We have to crap in a bag and then walk about 200 meters to the burn pit to dispose of it. Thankfully, someone had enough sense to build the burn pit on the leeward side of the base. Urine goes down urine tubes that disap-pear to God knows where. Showers are from a gravity fed pipe that is filled from well water. No one has ever told me how often, or how long we are allowed to shower, but I try to limit use as much as possible. We share the installation with some United Arab Emirates Special Forces, and they take too many showers. The chow hall is open 24/7, and meals are presented three times a day. Food is generally left out until the beginning of the next meal, so if you miss the official mealtime, you can always get a snack. There is an outside area cordoned off for a weight room, and another area set aside for cardio equipment. Running is limited to about a half-mile loop through the camp. We don't have any laundry machines, but I generally save the runoff from my shower and wash my clothes in that. It's not the most pleasant sounding habit, but I figure sweat diluted by a few gallons of water is better than sweat directly on the clothing. The neat thing is that, because it's so hot and dry here, clothes dry faster on the clothesline than they do in a dryer stateside. My room is an 8' X 8' plywood box with two outlets and an AC unit. I don't have to share that with anyone else, which is definitely nice. In theory, I should have internet in there, but it rarely works and when it does actually function it's slow. We have three MWR (Morale Welfare and Recrea-tion) computers in the chow hall, and they work fine most of the time. I get a fair amount of reading and writing done, so I enjoy that.

Steve

July 7th

Yesterday, a ring of IEDs trapped the guys in their vehicles for 10 hours before EOD finally cleared them. As a result, I ended up having to work till midnight instead of getting off around 1800, but I've been having easy days, so it was good to suffer a bit. I had to cancel class.

It's wonderful to watch Alba work with the kids. He really likes them, and while we both know they are full of it, when they come in complaining of specific diseases designed to pilfer expensive drugs, we usually send them off with Neosporin and vitamins. They know the price of some of the more exotic drugs, and their attempts to get them for free are well known. Today we had a boy come in with a headache, stomachache, and an undefined pain. I couldn't help but wonder if it was the same headache, stomachache, and undefined pain I used to get out of class in the 3rd grade. I have my suspicions. After we were done treating is imaginary symptoms, he began to have a list of family members who had lists of their own ailments. Alba said they should go see the village doctor, subsidized by the coalition, but if they couldn't they would have to come in person to the clinic for treatment. This was a rare opportunity for me. Normally, one of the three local-national interpreters would have done this, but they were busy elsewhere. Nothing pleases me more than being hauled out of bed to interact with the locals, and I wish I had more of it.

July 8th

I've been hanging out with Nick, the dog handler lately. He's a really nice guy with a very dark sense of humor. I still don't have much use for his dog, Hugo, who barks at me when I go take a piss. His cage is five meters from the tubes, and even though I know it's coming every time, I still flinch at the booming roar that echoes off the walls. Nick was hilarious when discussing the cop who died last week.

The police posts have been getting hit a lot lately. It's just harassment, but there have been a few small casualties; one guy was hit in the hip while taking a nap on the roof, and Billy is taking care of him.

July 9th

This is the point of a deployment where Groundhog Day* sets in. Normalcy becomes fatiguing. Some of the Afghan and US Army guys have gone up to some of the satellite installations for a few days, so I'm going to lose some of my students. Unfortunately, one of my best students is going on leave for a month, so I'll have some down time in the evenings.

I must be worn down, because three people have commented that I look tired; I feel fine though.

I've been doing some housekeeping lately to make my room a little nicer. I got a slab of thick heavy cardboard to put on the floor so I can walk with my shoes off inside without having my feet covered in dust. I've started "mopping" the floor with water left over from washing clothes. It's more like washing the dirt through gaps in the floor, but it decreases the dust, which would otherwise be in the air.

Dixie

The Army guys have brought back a stray dog who is named either "Dixie" or "Dog" depending on who is dealing with her. I'm taking her for walks in the evening to pass the time. She bites, but that's solved with a firm swat on the nose. I'm mentally preparing myself for Ramadan. If it negatively affects my ability to do my job, I'll stop immediately, but otherwise, I'll complete the exercise. My plan is to wake up at 0430 eat some chow, and go for a short walk while drinking water. Then, I'll go back to bed for a few hours before my shift starts.

*Termed Groundhog Day after the movie of the same name with Bill Murray in which he's repeating the same day over and over again.

July 10th

I'm upset at myself. Asad Ali has insisted on learning English, and I've tried, but he can't even read and write in Pashto or Dari. I've realized, after a few hours of teaching him, that there is no way I can teach him English without him being literate in Pashto or Dari. I'm upset, because I should have recognized my limitations and I've wasted my student's time.

Asad Ali and his brother, Mohammad Ali, are two of seven brothers and one sis-ter. Eight siblings in all, they are typical of the measurable results of 10 years of for-eign efforts to educate the populace. Asad Ali is 28, and he is illiterate in Dari though he cannot speak Pashto. Mohammad Ali is 22 and can read and write in both Pashto and Dari and is well on his way to functional English. Their younger brother, Ali, is a local-national interpreter fluent in Pashto, Dari, and English*. Asad Ali would have been approximately 18 at the time of our efforts here. It would have been largely too late for him to have benefited from the hundreds of schools that have been built throughout the country over the last ten years. Mohammad Ali on the other hand would have been 12, and he had the opportunity to go to some school, enough to have become fluent in an additional language and literate on his own. Pashto letters are similar to Dari letters, so his Pashto literacy could have been self-taught. Their younger brother, Ali, would have been eight, and therefore the beneficiary of 10 years of education. The younger the person, the more likely they have achieved functional literacy and other skills.

Despite constant threat of Taliban reprisal, attacks on schools and students, and the destruction of schools, the coalition and the Afghan government have shown a steadfast dedication to improving the literacy rate in Afghanistan, and more than 50 percent of the youth population is now enrolled in schools. We are rapidly approach-ing the tipping point of more Afghans being literate than illiterate.

We are not out of the woods on this issue. The literacy is disproportionately spread around the country and in gender. Areas like I, which avoided much of the Taliban intrusion prior to 9/11, were in the position to improve much more quickly than areas such as Helmand and Kandahar, where the Taliban is still present in the form of a shadow government.

*Not to be confused with Asad Ali, the Afghan-American interpreter previously mentioned.

July 12th

Any day now will be the official handover to Afghan forces for the city and province of Lashkar Gah. I predict there will be little violence in this city after coalition forces are gone. Over the next few months, we will see a slight pickup in IEDs in the province along with a few suicide bombings, but for the most part, it will be quiet. If I'm right, then this serves as litmus for the ability to eventually handover the whole country. If I'm wrong, then we've already lost, and it's time to go home anyway—we'll see.

Mohammad and Asad Ali, like most Hazara, are Shia Muslim. For all practical purposes, Shia and Sunni are identical, but a question over succession after Muhammad's death has created a rift that has lasted since the beginnings of the faith. With the exception of Iran, Iraq, and Lebanon, Shia make up a minority throughout the Islamic world, and while the two sects usually ignore each other, the waxing and waning of nationalistic furor often results in disenfranchisement and ethnic cleansing. Muhammad's nephew, Ali is highly revered among Shia muslims, and many have named their male children after him.

This explains how all seven brothers have Ali as their second name. Asad Ali, Mohammad Ali, Barak Ali, Sadiq Ali, Najib Ali, Karim Ali, and Qurban Ali. I suppose it's no worse than George Foreman naming his five sons George.

Mohammad is a very excitable guy, and after he listed his seven siblings, I added his sister Habiba and said, "Habiba Ali." Of course Ali is reserved only for males, and I know this, but Mohammad didn't realize that I'm teasing him, so he gets wide-eyed and says, "NO! Not Habiba Ali!"

I asked him to name all his brothers again, and at the end of it, I again say, "Habiba Ali." Mohammad is furious, and Asad Ali, knowing that I'm playing a joke falls off his mattress with laughter. I played the same joke on Mohammad one more time before he finally realized I was giving him a hard time.

July 13th

Hamid Karzai's brother, Wali Karzai was assassinated today. He was a physical example of the old guard, which relies on corruption and dirty dealing to get the job done. In the beginning that was necessary, because coercion and corruption is all anyone understood in this country, but 10 years in, he's been a great source of the continued strife in Kandahar. The same can be said for people like Rashid Dostum and the warlords who occupy parliament. We needed them at the time; we need new people now.

Hopefully, Karzai's replacement will be from the "new" Afghanistan.

I suspect Kandahar will see a slight rise in violence in the next six months, but by this time next year, overall violence will be down—in no small part because of this fel-low's demise. Good Riddance

I am putting greater effort into Asad Ali's literacy lessons, and I've enlisted his brother's help in this effort. Asad Ali is also taking his own initiative, and he has a notebook that he uses to copy the labels off food in the chow hall in both English and Dari.

Mohammad Ali, on the other hand is becoming more and more self-sufficient, and his supervisor, the cook has frequently commented on how much he has improved. My goal is to make Mohammad not only independent but also able to teach others.

July 15th

I have fleas. I don't know how I picked them up. I haven't been around any animals*, but low and behold, I have them. It's not hard to get rid of them, but it's a nuisance regardless. Removal is relatively simple; first, trim off as much body hair as possible with special emphasis placed on pubic hair. Wash the hair and body, dry off in open sunlight allowing the light to reach all sides of the body, apply copious amounts of talcum powder. This may need to be repeated for a couple days. Hopefully I don't get the plague.

*At the time of this writing, I had not made the obvious connection to the dog I'd been walking just a few days previously, but as I wrote it, I felt it necessary to keep it.

On the right, "It's possible that our children can have a better way." On the left, " Do not allow your children to go in this area. Report land mines to the national army or coalition forces."

July 18th

I worked till midnight and then hit the gym until 0100 after which I took a shower in the moonlight and retired to the hookah circle to enjoy some grape flavored tobacco—I love my job. Well, I at least love the location of my job and my time off after work.

July 19th

It's interesting how well people who have met me only once or twice treat me. I briefly interpreted for Sergeant Major Khan while a Camp Calero, and he is passing through Mirmandab. He waved me down and gave me a hearty greeting before introducing me to his commander and all of his troops. All of them were gracious and friendly, and they offered me tea. If I'm good enough for Sergeant Major Khan, then I'm good enough for them.

July 22nd

A PFC killed four guys with a grenade launcher two days ago. I asked him what he felt, and he said he felt nothing; training just kicked in. He hasn't been sleeping though, so I wonder if he's got issues he doesn't want to talk about.

Wahid, the Afghan medic is an outstanding student. He has been at another location for the last two weeks, but he's been studying on his own and is showing improvement. Students like Wahid are the easiest to work with, because they already have the basics of English down. I merely need to hone the skills they already have, and correct them when they make mistakes. The most difficult students are those like Asad Ali who have no foundation whatsoever.

July 23rd

There is another camp cleanup. The district governor is coming to the council, so it's a big deal with lots of extra security.

July 24th

Nick got an X-Ray to examine IEDs, and one of the guys is obsessively bugging him to X-Ray his knee, which was hurt before the deployment. He pushed through it to avoid being dumped from the rotation. It is commonplace in all services for people to put off medical treatment, because they are afraid of the short-term ramifications.

July 25th

We had a laugh the other night when EOD Nick freaked out as two fighting cats burst through the hookah area and he was about to fall out of his chair. Loud noises are always startling in such a quiet place, but as an EOD guy, he's particularly on edge.

This place is starting to feel like a prison. The walls and the concertina wire aren't far off from being in a Department of Corrections facility back home.

[Short Essay on an Evening "Out"]

The power went out tonight. I suppose it's more accurate to say that the generator came to life, provided energy for a few moments then sputtered to a stop. It wouldn't give a reading as to why it failed to remain on, so the only thing to do was start it over and over again and hope for a miracle. One can't plan an evening around circular power outages; so, it's sit alone in the dark or go for a walk. I chose the latter.

I meandered toward the burn pit to deposit the day's leavings. I stumbled twice. Ruts left behind in the rainy season harden into brick, and a casual step after dark can twist or break and ankle, but luckily I was just mildly embarrassed. I doubt anyone saw, except perhaps, a lone watchman with night vision.

After a few moments of pause to watch the flames of the burn pit, I walked out to the rifle range and decided to take advantage of an evening without lights. Stargazing. So many in America have no idea what it feels like to look up at the stars without the influence of the city. Even 10 or 20 miles away from a metropolitan area, the light still interferes with the clear viewing of the heavens. It is a humbling experience, and in the few moments taken to look at the grandeur of the galaxy puts everything in perspective and it's an almost religious clarity that asserts, nothing matters all that much.

I just lay in the gravel on my back for a few minutes. It might have been five minutes, maybe thirty; I lost track of time. I was facing south, but tilting my head slightly back and to the west, I could see the Big Dipper pointing the way to the North Star. We're in the northern hemisphere, so the stars are the same as "back home." Corresponding with those that have never had the chance or taken the chance to just watch the stars are those that have never seen a falling meteor. Here, one need only pause for a few minutes. I saw one streaking in a southeasterly direction, and in an odd synchrony, one of the towers shot off a flare. I lingered for a few minutes and ignored the first half-dozen mosquito bites. Then I went back inside and fell asleep in my sweltering but gradually cooling room, with no power.

July 26th

It's almost comical in its own way that Gulab Mangal, the Helmand governor, was attacked on his way to the funeral of Wali Karzai, the former Kandahar governor. Gulab Mangal is a good governor, by Afghan standards, so it's good to see that he has survived his third attack in as many months.

There is a certain admiration I have to have for these folks who continually face their own demise while running the nation. Of course, I know they have their own ambitions and it's simply the risk that is involved, but there are cases where locals stand up to the Taliban and have little to gain in the short-term. One man was recently black mailed by Taliban who had kidnapped his son, and when he refused to turn over his police vehicle, they killed his son. He's still working.

July 29th

I might go to Camp Bastion for a couple days in the next few weeks. I'll get a real shower and be able to wash my laundry in a proper facility. I'll also get the rest of my stuff, which includes some badly needed extra socks. I came here under the impression that I was only here for two weeks, so I am short on clothing, socks, and hygiene products.

Ali is leaving; he's pathetic—so pathetic that he's not even staying for his six-month mark and faking a mental breakdown, in which he claimed he was going to grab Mark's gun and shoot himself. He's been moaning for weeks about his 16-year old son's claim to "need his daddy," but everyone is confused at how he is suddenly so needed merely four months into the deployment. I might room with Asad after Ali is gone. I'll have to pick up some of Ali's duties to lighten the load on Asad, but he truly didn't do much, so it won't be a big deal.

Fingers was ogling the Marines while they worked out today while laying out on a cot in the sun like a swimsuit model. He's a flaming homosexual even by Afghan standards. I find it a bit funny.

I'm dreading abstaining from caffeine during Ramadan. It's not forbidden, but I don't think I can realistically stay hydrated if I'm drinking the stuff.

One of the Marines made an interesting point about modern war; he said war has gotten too easy, and we need to have horrible gut wrenching warfare that makes people avoid it as much as possible.

I'm going to insulate my room tomorrow.

July 30th

There has been a significant drop in violence over the last few days; I think most of the fighters are headed home for Ramadan.

I insulated my room today, but while doing so, I managed to breathe a bunch of fiberglass into my lungs—I'm an idiot. The rooms only have a single sheet of plywood in between each other, and there are a couple places where light slips through, and I can hear every sound of my neighbors. All I had to do was track down some old insulation and some discarded plywood to alleviate the situation.

July 31st

I'm working on buying my tickets to go home in October. I should be able to go for ~3 weeks.

There are approximately 50 coalition deaths this month—an average monthly total based on trends that is down significantly from last year's total of 88.

1.   O you who have believed, do not approach prayer while you are intoxicated until you know what you are saying or in a state of janabah, except those passing through [a place of prayer], until you have washed [your whole body]. And if you are ill or on a journey or one of you comes from the place of relieving himself or you have

 contacted women and find no water, then seek clean earth and wipe over your faces and your hands [with it]. Indeed, Allah is ever Pardoning and Forgiving. Surah 4:43

4

AUGUST

[Pre-Ramadan Essay]

Ramadan is rapidly approaching. It's one of the five pillars of Islam, a requirement to refrain from eating, drinking, and sex during the day.

It is similar to Lent in Roman Catholic tradition as a time for prayer, reflection,
and sacrifice, but it is also similar in that the pre and post debauchery for the average
adherent more than makes up for the abstinence. While the Catholics cram 40-days of
abstinence into the weeks leading up Ash Wednesday, the Muslims tend to make a

small party out of each evening's break of the fast. It's not uncommon for a penitent Muslim to gorge himself, vomit, and gorge again; when the fast is finished, they have three day celebration with gift-giving, singing, and dancing. It is more low-key than Mardi Gras, but still enormous.

Breaking fast

I've decided to try fasting this year. As the holy month of Ramadan is based on the lunar calendar used in the Islamic world, the shorter months of the lunar cycle mean that Ramadan shifts to the left by approximately 11 days each year. This is my third and final attempt at this exercise having failed in previous attempts. If I succeed on this venture, I will have completed one of the most difficult months of fasting. As fasting times are determined by sunrise and sunset, the longer days of summer mean longer fasting times. Thankfully I'm on the good side of the solstice, so the length of the day will decrease slightly as the month goes on. A small comfort but I'll take it.

I'm not Muslim. Because I'm an American, Afghans assume I'm Christian or Jewish, which despite the perceived difference in the media, are quite similar and most the Abrahamic traditions are respected and tolerated by the average Muslim.

Islam is hard to like, but that's mostly because of the followers. Not only do they wish to proselytize non-Muslims, but the lack of free thought prevents more liberal interpretation of Koranic verse. I do think we are on the cusp of an Islamic reformation, which will be a dawning of liberal ideals, but in the meantime, I am a bit impatient with the rhetoric of Muslims I deal with on a regular basis. However, I am driven by curiosity and a desire to understand diverse cultures. Of course, I'm sure there will be nothing exciting about bulldozing through the days without the benefit of coffee or a full stomach. Workouts will be relegated to the night hours if they are done at all, and

I'll be hitting a siesta every afternoon. Interestingly enough, I'll cut weight just in time for the 10-year high school reunion that I can't go to. I'm sure I'll be missed. I don't have a scale to know how much I weigh, and it would be nice to do a pre-Ramadan and post-Ramadan comparison, but that's not possible. I'll just try to chronicle how I look and feel each day and leave it at that.

Cheating would serve no purpose, though it is common among Muslims who will sneak a bite to eat or a sip of water. I have had numerous Muslims confess to me in private, "everyone does it." With a sidelong look to ensure no one can hear them, they confess to fooling their neighbor, but I've never asked them how they feel about fool-ing an omniscient God.

I'm going to do my best not to cheat. It will only take away from the overall experience, omniscient God and nosy neighbors aside.

August 1st

Ramadan is here; today is the first day of fasting. I got a nice sense of light-headed euphoria about halfway through the day that felt like hypoxia. The bulk of my work was finished, so I took a nap. I haven't craved caffeine as much as I thought I would, but there is a dull ache behind the euphoria that is probably a symptom of caffeine withdrawal.

My random musings are worse than usual, and I am wondering if drug addicts could be treated in a manner similar to what happens in Ramadan. If they were concentrating on hunger, they might not notice the missing drugs. I suspect they would be so malnourished, that they would die from the trauma.

I'm being teased by a few Marines who say if I want to know the culture better I should fuck a guy. It's more efficient than a month of fasting. No thanks.

Asad wants me to go pray with him, but I don't want to. I want an authentic experience, but I do think it would be improper for me to intrude as a non-Muslim interloper.

August 2nd

It's the second day of Ramadan, and the headaches haven't come back. I think I might have broken the fast 15 minutes early yesterday. The imam was doing his prayer call, but it was still bright outside.

August 3rd

I got my tickets today. I'll be on leave from October 18th to November 9th.

I had a really interesting chat with John, a Christian, who among other things, believed in a new earth and didn't believe in evolution, which he said was a lie and a waste of tax dollars. His explanation for dinosaur bones was, "it's interesting that every society on earth has dragons somewhere in their mythology; those bones are dragon bones not dinosaur bones." I declined arguing with him, because I enjoyed listening to some really "out there" justifications for taking the biblical creation story seriously. For example he had explanations for everything, including the ozone thinning as a reason why humans no longer live to be 900 years old. "It's all right there in the creation story, you just have to read it," he insisted. He's a really nice guy, so I didn't criticize his views and in a way, the conversation was very enlightening. We traded a few books.

It feels bizarre to talk about Christian philosophy with a new-earth adherent in an archly conservative Muslim society while fasting for Ramadan as a non-Muslim. Maybe I'm hungry.

August 4th

I've decided to move in with Asad; he is one of the most obnoxious people I've ever met, but I can put up with a lot if it means having an internet cord. For some reason, the cords in his area work, and in my area they don't. I'm still amazed that there is internet at all in such an austere location.

I'm still teaching class to Mohammad Ali and Asad Ali. I go to their room after they break the fast, but I only have a few minutes of time to work with them. They have shifted much of their duties around in order to accommodate sleeping as much as possible during the day. I won't be working with the soldiers for Ramadan, which makes my life a lot less complicated but eliminates a huge source of distraction for me. I will miss the classes, but Mohammad Ali is such a great student regardless.

August 5th

Mail Day! I've been going a bit crazy waiting for something from home. I ordered a bird book several weeks ago, and it's finally arrived. In addition, I have five packages from friends stateside. I have requested classroom materials from some friends stateside in addition to some items for myself.

I've had a very bad sore throat lately, so I'm going to be more proactive about drinking orange juice. It will probably only help as a placebo, but that's fine.

I've also gotten backed up from not drinking enough water because of fasting. I guess constipation is one of the mysterious health benefits the Muslims keep telling me about.

They will have to put Dixie down, because she is a risk to the working dogs and to the people here. The biggest issue is parvo, a contagious canine virus, which could wipe out the working dogs. She has also not been vaccinated for Rabies, and Afghanistan is a hotbed for rabies infections. As of now, no one has contracted it but bites are common.

[Letter Home: August 5th]

Howdy Parents,

I haven't written in quite some time, so hello.

I decided to do the Ramadan fast this year. There are a handful of reasons to do it, but the predominant reason is just to better understand the culture. I've always been curious what makes societies tick. The second reason is to break up the monotony a little bit. Frankly, it's just something to do. The third reason is that my co-worker will complain constantly if he's the only one fasting, so I figure if I am doing it, I can tell him to "shut the fuck up" when he starts whining.

It's not terribly hard. No eating, drinking, smoking, or sex from sunup to sundown. I suppose it would suck in an Alaskan summer. Here it lasts from ~0430 to ~1930, so 15 hours. Fortunately, the days will get slightly shorter.

I'll grant that it's less than an hour's difference but psychologically, setting the alarm a few minutes later each day is nice. I get up at 0330 and eat around 700 calories while drinking as much water as I can hold. Then, I sleep to 1000 and start my shift, which lasts till 1800 on most days. I'll goof off for about an hour, check email, and pass the time.

Hunger has never really bothered me, but I have grown accustomed to about three quarts of water each day, so not drinking for 15 hours... I get by. I don't smoke, and I haven't seen a female for almost a month, so those parts won't be hard.

After a half a day of not eating, the body starts pumping the endorphins. I think this is why anorexia becomes so addictive; eating stops the endorphins. Maybe [endorphins] caused visions for whatever Stone Age culture you'd like to discuss. Of course, visions also require sleep deprivation, and I'm getting plenty of that.

I am getting a mild buzz and a tiny headache, but I think that is a side effect of cutting coffee rather than a fasting-related ailment.

I haven't noticed any detrimental effects other than the glare of a Christian zealot. He probably thinks I'm converting.

That's all for now.

Steve

August 8th

Billy said that if Dixie could stay on the army side of the compound, he'd ignore her.

Another dog handler has arrived as a replacement for Dog-Handler Nick. Dog Handler Chris's dog is far nicer than Hugo.

A Chinook crashed the other day; the Taliban are claiming responsibility, but I doubt it. It has been reported that 30 were killed.

Tonight was a huge success. I taught present and future progressive tenses to Mohammad Ali. I have taken him farther than any other student at this point. I would have eventually taught Habibullah the concept of progressives, but I left before I could get that far.

August 9th

I ripped ass last night, and it sounded like automatic gunfire. Asad sat up in bed and asked if we were getting attacked.

I've continued teaching during the fast, but I am waiting till the evening, and I'm only working with Asad Ali and Mohammad. Asad Ali was able to read out loud in Dari, "I read Dari." If I can get him to a level where he can write, "I write Dari," I'll feel I've taught him something. Mohammad's grasp of English has continued to sky-rocket, and his supervisor, the army cook, has thanked me repeatedly for working with him. As of now, I've taught him all the simple and progressive tenses, but I haven't taught him things like participles and conditionals yet. He is going on leave soon, so I'll lose my student, but I believe that he's self-sufficient now and I am merely a guide.

I broke fast with the Arabs last night. As typical for anytime I've been around Arabs, they waste more food than they eat. The main food was goat, rice, some kind of meat dumping, and the highlight of the beverages was the Barbicans, non-alcoholic malt beverages, that taste like a cider or grape soda depending on the variety. Most importantly, they had fresh vegetables, of which we've had a severe shortage for some time.

August 10th

There are rumors of corpse mutilation by a Brit. What a dumb thing to do.

Tonight I broke fast with the workers on the Arab side. The workers are an eclectic mix. Just like any other wealthy country, the United Arab Emirates has its share of immigrants, but unlike the American military, the UAE military brings them along for cheap labor. Also unlike America, immigrants are unable to become full citizens, but for simplicity, I will use a hyphenated system familiar in the US. The cook is a Pakistani-Emirati and the rest of the workers including two interpreters are Afghan-Emirati. Their socioeconomic class is far lower than that of their UAE employers and as with most members of lower socioeconomic classes, their behavior tends to be less refined. The meal was punctuated by raucous Urdu and Pashto music, pseudo-homosexual fondling, and a cruder cuisine consisting of incredibly tough goat meat topped off with the head of the goat fried and placed over rice. Asad grimaced at the workers peeling flesh from the face of the goat and to bring him back down to earth they chased him around the room with the decapitated head while he shrieked for them to stop. Anytime one can make Asad feel uncomfortable, it's a good day. I'm going to eat on the Arab side every other night. Generally, I'll eat with the workers who are Pakistani and Afghan, but periodically, I'll dine with the Arabs. I can speak Pashto or Dari with the workers, and while I can't respond to the Pakistani, I can at least understand what he says when he speaks Urdu. I can't speak Arabic, so eating with the

Arabs can be lonely. The good thing about the Arabs is that they have a very good setup for their MWR, and while I don't miss TV, it will be nice to see a few Gator games this fall. I'm curious to see how they do with a new head coach.

No luck on saving Dixie. I tried chaining her on the other side of base and walking her several times a day, but she barks all night, and the soldiers untie her. The next morning, she's back over here.

Noroz dance

Euthanasia is quick and painless. An M9 at point blank range doesn't leave many nerve endings to worry about.

A bunch of bad guys got killed yesterday. I guess it's sort of revenge for the 30 dead Americans in the Chinook crash. Eight Afghans also died and at least one working dog.

[Letter Home: August 10th]

Parents,

I've begun to break the fast with the Muslims every other evening. I probably won't continue after Ramadan.

We share the compound with a few dozen soldiers from the UAE and a handful of Afghan and Paki workers. The UAE are better supplied than us, so tonight I was greeted with a giant tray of fresh fruit. In the American chow hall I haven't seen anything but Granny Smith Apples for weeks, and they had fruit I had never even seen be-fore. One was called "basha'a" in Arabic, and I never caught the name of the other. Basha'a looks like a sea urchin, and inside there is an opaque gelatinous fruit that tastes vaguely like muscadine grapes. The other fruit looked like green Japanese Persimmons. Tonight they had chicken kabobs on saffron rice. They don't use utensils, but instead, they shred the chicken with one hand, mix it in with the communal rice plate, and finally make a ball of rice with their fist, which is shoved into their mouths. So far, I haven't had much success with the rice ball. It's probably a failure to commit 100 percent to shoving my hand all the way in—kind of like a mousetrap only hurts when you are hesitant. I don't think I'll ever get used to communal food.

I only go to the Muslim side of base every-other night, because I lift weights in the evening, and I don't like lifting on a full stomach. Even though I've spent all day fasting, I still hit the gym while slowly ingesting a liter of diluted Gatorade. The reality is that I'll be taking in close to 1,000 calories in a very short time, and I don't want to move after that. I've embraced not being able to run in this compound, and though I've never terribly liked lifting weights, it will be good for me. It still doesn't compare to running 15-20 miles with a rucksack and some water bottles.

I'll stop going to the Muslim chow hall when Ramadan concludes. The purpose of experiencing another culture will have ceased, and I'll just feel like an interloper. I'm not Muslim; I'll never be Muslim. However, it would be funny to say, "I converted, because the food was better."

My roommate was describing how to pray properly, and he specified proper placement of three fingers of the right hand on the wrist of the left hand, and when I asked why it was important, he didn't know, so he asked some of the Arabs who had no idea what he was talking about. So he and his family have been praying a certain way for generations, but he (and his family) had no idea why. He ended up making up some bullshit about how his way forces you to concentrate on god.

I don't see anything "wrong" with the religion other than the fact that it has entirely too many rules. Free will is not a concept that has been adopted so far in Islam, though I feel that the time of a reformation is rapidly approaching. In the meantime, I don't care to be told that I'm standing wrong when I pray, from some jackass who knows nothing of his own religion. That's really the crux of my aversion to any organized religion. It's not the religion, but the simple-minded minions who are attracted to it.

I'll just do my best to keep my mouth shut and enjoy the food. I'm only good at one of those.

Steve

August 11th

I had dinner with the Arabs again. It was gorgeous chicken kabobs and rice. I actually feel like I've gained weight.

Cowboy has been fired for repeatedly sleeping while on the job. Fingers is incredibly industrious, but Cowboy is regularly caught being lazy and has to be pushed to work. His English has improved dramatically since I've worked with him, so I suspect he will have no trouble finding a job. He's only 19 and surprisingly immature for a 19-year old Afghan. I think this will be a learning experience for him.

August 12th

There is talk about putting in some flush toilets. Some of the guys have been digging out a hole, but I don't know when it will be completed.

We got gravel delivered today. It will be a lot more pleasant with the main driveways and courtyard being covered. I'll still have to trudge through a foot of dust to get rid of the wag bags, but at least walking to and from work and the chow hall will be eas-ier.

August 13th

We had a scorpion pay us a visit in the room last night. It just walked right past us while we were watching a movie. I caught it and put it in a water bottle, but evidently the small amount of water in the bottom of the bottle caused him to burst from over hydration. I looked at pictures, and he looks like one of the really dangerous ones, but I can't be sure.

August 15th

I had been told that fasting causes strange dreams, and last night, I had my first Ramadan dream. In the dream I was sneaking food. For some reason there were a bunch of Valentine's Day hearts in a bag outside, and as I grabbed a handful and shoved them in my mouth, Chad caught me and yelled at me.

I did have to cheat yesterday, because I was unable to sleep the entire night before, and as I planned, if it was going to affect the mission, I'd have to eat. I didn't eat breakfast, but I did have some coffee and a little water halfway through the day to keep me going.

August 16th

Trying to work out while fasting is interesting. I did legs yesterday, which has left me exhausted but feeling pretty positive.

Eid slaughter

August 17th

There is a huge, stray dog hanging around the camp; his name is Tiger. He is well over 100 pounds, and it makes me reluctant to go out at night, because he hangs out by the burn pit. Another ALP guy that was friends with Asad was killed yesterday. He was shot six times to the head and torso, and there wasn't enough left of him to even patch up. Billy was joking about it. The angle of the bullet caused the jaw to snap open in an unnatural position, and he said that all he could think about was Megan Fox in "Jennifer's Body." "Now I want to fuck Megan Fox," he said. His humor is always morbid. He's seen so much death and he's survived at least two explosions.

Eid al-Fitr is really right around the corner. The moon is waning.

August 19th

While I am disappointed to receive a box of Christian literature when I was hop-ing for classroom material and some stuff for the locals, I am sure that I'll enjoy read-ing Dinosaurs and the Bible. I couldn't even write the title "Dinosaurs and the Bible" without my abs cramping up from laughter.

August 20th

We've chopped the monster's head off for a few weeks with the capture of a mid-level commander in the area.

It might be time to shave the beard; one of the Afghans jokingly asked me if I was joining the Taliban.

I was shocked to find out that Mohammad Ali has read the Bible. They covered it as a part of history in his schooling. He hasn't read the whole thing, but he said he's read excerpts of it. I was picking through a stack of greeting cards in the chow hall and was explaining what they were. He was able to name the characters of the nativity scene shown on the front cover of one of the cards.

August 21st

There is a super mouse hanging out in my room. By super mouse, I mean he can leap about 4 feet into the air. Asad wants to smack him with a boot. I'm more of a live and let live kind of dude, so I've removed all the food from the room and therefore, in theory, his desire to be here.

This mouse is too much of a bad ass to kill. Asad threw a water bottle at him today and the mouse just stared him down.

August 22nd

Asad is bugging me to pick up the slack left from Ali, but he only does 6 hours of work on most days, and I'm already doing 8-12. I think he just gets lonely by himself and wants the company; I did a shift for him, and he hung around. Finally, I had to say to him that if I was going to work part of his shift, he had to leave, because I wanted peace and quiet. He refused to leave, so I told him to do his own job and walked out.

I had to break my fast early for the second time today. Finger's brother-in-law has replaced Cowboy as a laborer and I find him hard to like. He was critical of my breaking the fast, and Finger's jumped to my defense and said that I was just doing it for the experience. I was told by the brother in law that deliberately breaking the fast means having to fast for 60 days instead of 30, but this is a common misconception in the Islamic world and has no basis in the Koran which simply says you have to make the day up later. He is unable to read and write, and like so much of the Islamic world, he's at the mercy of an Imam who often is illiterate as well.

[Letter Home: August 22nd]

Dear Jasmine,

Regarding my comments on history judging [President George W.] Bush in a very positive light. I think the Arab spring is in huge part due to the catalyst provided by a fledgling and theoretically successful democracy in Iraq. While certainly not the first democracy in the Middle East/North Africa, it was the certainly the one that demonstrated the possibility of fractured Muslim populations being able to actually engage in civic discussion, without killing each other. Certainly he screwed up in dealing with Iran, but while isolating Iran, he furthered the peace process in Israel/Palestine. Of course, that peace was subject to the same on again off again issues faced by every president since Carter.

He was the first president to really push the Sudan issue. While he hardly solved the Darfur conflict, he did play a huge role in the, so far, relatively peaceful partition of Southern Sudan, which will set the precedent for other splits.

He continued integration and cooperation with NAFTA as well as China and South America.

Internationally, I find his misunderstanding of insurgencies in places like Somalia frustrating, and the refusal to recognize grassroots democracy at its finest (Hamas) was hypocritical, but you can't please everyone all the time.

He caused gratuitous strife with Russia over the missile defense shield, but by doing so he paved the way for a more comprehensive missile defense system which may or may not be needed depending on how things go in the future.

You can't really blame the economic collapse on him. The system was fractured to begin with, and the Bush tax cuts did nothing except expose those weaknesses sooner rather than later. Also, his bailouts are all part of the liberal economic theory that has guided our nation through plenty of recessions before this, so he was simply following the status quo. On the domestic front, I'd say the three unforgiveable things would be: failing to charge detainees with a crime, failing to treat them as prisoners of war and pushing for the Patriot Act. Right or wrong, those issues worked themselves out within a decade, and while there are still uncharged detainees in Gitmo, they are truly the worst of the bunch, and one by one the rest were repatriated. The bad stuff in the Patriot Act was also struck down eventually.

I stand by my statement, that history will likely look very kindly on Bush. If you read your history book, you'll recognize that Lincoln and Roosevelt did many of the same things, and history looked very kindly on them too.

I will concede to one thing. Should the western world not come out of our current slump, then he will be viewed pretty dimly, but I expect we'll be just fine.

Steve

August 23rd

I saw one of the most bizarre things today in regards to Islamic culture. Some of the guys from the UAE were using our gym, and the guy doing power cleans was yelling Allah-u-Akbar (god is great) on every repetition. Allah-u-Akbar is commonly shouted before and after a successful attack, but it is strange to see it used during a weight lifting routine—oh well.

My bed is becoming more and more unstable; Ali built it for a guy who weighed 130, and I'm close to 180. He also didn't use enough reinforcements. I figure I'll just wait for it to collapse before I fix it, which should be in a few days.

August 24th

I guess the bed wasn't going to last a few more days; at 0200, the whole thing shifted sideways and I tumbled out. I fixed it before I went to work.

I ran into some concertina wire that was surrounding some of the buildings and jutting out into the pathway. I have gashes on my right shin in three places. At least I wasn't wearing pants. My pants would have been destroyed; my leg will grow back.

Mohammad departed for his home in Herat a few days ago, and that means that I've been spending more time with Asad Ali. They haven't always lived in Herat, but after the Taliban in Oruzgan killed an uncle, they decided to leave the area for a more peaceful part of the country. Herat is very liberal by Afghan standards, and one of the handful of Afghan female politicians is from Herat. Asad Ali has a visceral dislike of Pashtuns and even takes time to describe Fingers as a bully who mistreats him. I wonder how many generations it will take for this type of feeling to fade.

August 25th

There are four days left of Ramadan; I doubt I'll do it again.

August 26th

The Taliban were shooting during the break of fast last night, and the Afghan in-terpreter for the Arabs started swearing and complaining that the Taliban did not re-spect Islam or Islamic traditions.

August 28th

I did some laundry today. We can share the Arab washing machines, but they are fickle and often in use by the Arabs, so I continue to do it by hand. It's not difficult and it's a good exercise that saves water. I think I will try to wash my clothes by hand in the US when I have time, because I like to conserve water and energy. I have a small garbage can that I use to collect dripping water from our air conditioner. I put a few items of clothing in the garbage pail to reduce the sound of the dripping water, because it is annoying when we try to sleep. With clothes in the pail, it takes about one day to fill up with water. After that, I put in a few tablespoons of laundry detergent, swish the clothing around in the water for a few minutes, and then let it soak. After it has soaked for perhaps an hour, I dump the water out and take the trash can to the shower where I fill it up again, swish the clothes around to rinse them, and then I hang them up on a clothes line. As I've said before, it's very dry here, so clothes take less than two hours to dry.

August 29th

Go figure that the last day of Ramadan is the hardest. I didn't sleep last night, but I'm not going to cheat on this, the last day. I want to finish strong.

One of the guys is getting sent home for malaria—rough country. I haven't been taking my doxycycline for weeks now, but I think I'll start again, nothing like someone else's tragedy to straighten me out.

August 30th

There are Eid celebrations today; even the Taliban are not shooting. If the next two days remain quiet, August deaths will just barely top last year's totals, and that's with the helicopter crash, the most deadly day on record.

Ramadan is over. I will begin eating normally tomorrow.

[Post-Ramadan Commentary]

Ramadan has concluded. While I wasn't expecting some spiritual transformation during my participation in the month-long fast; I was only hoping to have a greater understanding of the culture that subjects itself to this every single year except in specific times such as extreme illness or while taking the Hajj.

I had mixed results.

The quickest remark of a Muslim when defending the custom is to extoll the "health benefits" of fasting. When pressed on specific health benefits, they shift the argument to the fact many doctors have said fasting is healthy. When asked which doctors, they continue to sidestep the question. As with most ardently faithful adherents to any religion, a truly logical and coherent argument never actually arises. I will offer the tangible results of my experience with the fast.

Prior to Ramadan, I was able to keep my resting heart rate down around 60bpm. It wasn't stellar, but given the circumstances, it was good enough. I've checked it five times since the end of the fast just to make sure I wasn't mistaken, and I'm averaging 72bpm now. I am definitely worse off for cardiovascular fitness. I have probably lost a few pounds, but my metabolism sank so low during the day, that when cramming 1,000-1,500 calories of fatty food during the evening rush, I've gained huge swathes of pudgy bulbous fat on my legs, buttocks, and hips. I don't have a method to measure my blood pressure, but based on the sleepy sensations I've been getting, I believe my pressure is up. Obviously, some of my physical strength and endurance has been reduced due to lack of exercise. I did my best to maintain some level of physical fitness during this time, but I could only manage so much. I did greatly reduce my dependency on caffeine during this time period, but beyond that, I cannot confirm any health benefits.

My only real explanation for purported health benefits is that those who tend to live to excess on a daily basis would benefit from allowing their bodies and/or minds to rest and reset. If you're an obese glutton, you would likely lose weight during Ramadan. If you're an addict of any sort, you would likely loosen the bonds of your addiction. If you're a poor reader, enthusiastic study of the Koran (which I did not do) would allow you to strengthen your intellect; the possibilities continue. The point is that for those who already strive to lead a life of moderation, the fast is merely a speed bump, and the benefits would be balanced out by the deficiencies.

In reality, I suspect that Muslims don't do it for health reasons. They do it because they believe they have been commanded to do so by God; no other justification should be necessary, unless one wishes for a lively debate on belief in the intangible.

I did get a first-hand view of the culture. I interacted closely with the Afghans in a manner I could never have duplicated in a classroom. I'm thankful for that opportunity. As far as any other benefits to the ritual, I can find none, and I doubt I shall participate again.

[Letter Home: August 30th]

Claude,

I finally had the chance to do some real bird watching. I got my bird book halfway through Ramadan, and I didn't want to go outside during the day while fasting.

We are surrounded by walls and razor wire, but while standing in a guard tower I can see out. It is a very limited field of view, but I'll manage. This morning, I found Western Marsh Harrier, Variable Wheatear, and European Magpie. I've also done some research on some earlier birds and my total comes to eleven, including: Common Myna, House Sparrow, Alpine Swift, European Roller, Common Quail, Long

Tailed Shrike, Laughing Dove, and Barn Swallow. Of course eleven species would take 20 minutes in the US, but I'm happy with my modest list, given the conditions.

The Variable Wheatear reminds me of a Black Phoebe in size, color, and stature, but it doesn't fly catch. The Marsh Harrier flaps about in large uncoordinated wing beats like a Common Crow, and it seems like he can barely fly at all. He has a cream colored forehead which continues down the neck halfway down the leading edge of the wings, though at 200 meters, I could only see the forehead. The European Magpie is like any other magpie species. I will hopefully be traveling next week and double my count. An uneducated and random goal is 100 birds in my year here. My field guide to the birds of the Middle East does not have range maps beyond Iran, so I have to confirm using the wiki page of Afghan birds. I'll also get a guide to the birds of India which will also likely not have range maps for Afghanistan, but, not counting coastal birds, I think it's safe to assume that if a bird is found in both Iran and India, it will also be found in Afghanistan.

I'm really enthusiastic about my idea for an Afghan-specific book.

I have to bird with a Kevlar helmet and body armor, which is amusing. I stand up for a few moments at a time, but I consult the field guide from a seated position. Snipers rarely engage us, but I don't intend to be the next victim.

I think an article about birding in Afghanistan would be funny. Between dodging land mines in Bagram and dodging snipers in Helmand, someone would laugh.

Steve

August 31st

With over 80 deaths, August 2011 will be the deadliest month on record for America. For the coalition as a whole it ranks as number three. The deadliest month was June of last summer, the only month in the entire campaign that has seen more than 100 coalition deaths. The second deadliest month on record was July of last year.

I'll be going to Bagram to do some paperwork. I need the break.

5

SEPTEMBER

September 2nd

I'm traveling to Bagram and I won't be coming back to VSP Mirmandab. I'll miss my students.

At first, I grabbed a rucksack and a sleeping bag for some temporary travel, but after later information trickled down, I had 45 minutes to unpack and repack four duffle bags worth of gear for permanent transfer to Forward Operating Base (FOB) Robinson. I can't believe this is new information, and I hate being left in the dark on something like this. I spent my little remaining time taking pictures and saying goodbye.

I'll fly to Bagram tomorrow or the day after—maybe.

Strangely enough, Mia was at Mirmandab with two female medical personnel. I gave her a bear hug, but I was sprinting toward the convoy, so I didn't have any time to talk.

September 3rd

I'll make it to Bagram today or tomorrow. I'm being routed through KAF, so it will depend on my connecting flight.

The climate control in the Bastion terminal is incredibly inefficient in this heat. The AC is blasting full speed, but it only affects the area directly in front of the vent. Without ventilation up top, the super-heated air has nowhere to go.

September 4th

KAF smells just like it did last time. Fortunately, I'll be sleeping on the opposite side of the base from the Shit Pond, so I'll only smell it when the wind blows hard.

I spotted a new bird today and confirmed two others I had previously seen. The Afghan Babbler [bird] is aptly named.

I spent the morning reading while waiting for a trip to the terminal. The MWR is a 2-minute sprint and a 5 to 6-minute jog from the terminal, so I went to send a quick email and grab some KFC for the guy who was watching my gear while I ran, but neither of us made the flight anyway. Contractors are always on a space available basis, which means if a uniformed soldier comes along; the seat you reserved is taken. I'll spend another day meandering around, birding, and sightseeing.

I've had numerous senior NCOs tell me that a whining soldier is a happy soldier; a soldier who doesn't complain is going to hurt himself or others. That being said, I am amused at the absurdity of some complaints, including the fact that the new icecream machine would not be installed until the winter, so they wouldn't get to enjoy it; war is hell.

I'm going to grab a one-hour nap and go exploring.

[Letter Home: September 4th]

Parents,

I've got to take a few days to travel to Bagram Air Field, and when I'm done, I'll be headed to a different FOB. I'll be doing the same job.

I'm currently at KAF. It's a festering over-crowded shithole, and I'd rather be back on my FOB.

This is the center of ISAF, which is the UN's experiment on managing a coalition with forty member nations. The results are mixed. Joint command often sacrifices unity, and a multitude of chiefs with not enough Indians means no one ever gets anything done. Each country has its own rules of engagement and interpretation of international law, which means controlled chaos. A rare compliment from me on anything is they are doing the best they can, and I think this is a learning experience for future attempts at nation building.

I think the only real mistake is allowing so many countries to contribute warfighting capabilities. Of course now, the mistake has been remedied, but the first few years had people engaging in fighting who were completely unqualified. The unfair reality is, that of the coalition, there are only a few countries that are experts at war fighting, and those who can't or won't do what must be done, sometimes hold them back. Obviously, the US has the most experience, but there are other "experts" including the British, Aussies, French, and Koreans. While it sucks for the casualty burden to have fallen mostly on the backs of US, British, and French troops, it is how it must be; this allows other nations to bring their own capabilities to the table.

Perhaps the best example of this would be the rich Arab states. They have the money and the capability to build roads, schools, and mosques; however, the only gun they should be trusted with is a caulking gun. After my limited exposure to UAE troops, my only observation was to note that they put the "special" in Special Forces. They were overweight sloths, and I'd bet a week's pay on a platoon of ANA regulars,

against the finest the UAE has to offer. However, the UAE Special Forces did help construct a mosque a bazaar and a highway through Mirmandab. By doing so, they put a Muslim face on a predominantly Western occupation; they built rapport while the US killed insurgents and trained police. That's the type of division of labor we need to see more of. Countries with a history of mine clearing should clear mines; countries with robust medical infrastructure should build hospitals, etc.

As I stated, this is being done NOW, but I don't think the division of labor was al-ways so effective.

Steven

September 5th

I don't have a flight till this evening, so I'm going to get a feel for the place by riding the bus to the far side of base and seeing the sites. The AC on the bus didn't work, and everyone was dripping with sweat; the windows don't open.

It's interesting to see mangled war wreckage that is usually heaped in a pile out on the outskirts of a base. Humvees, MRAPs, and other assorted vehicles which have been blown apart get towed and left.

Kandahar is far more humid than Helmand, but it's still very dry. Clothing that took 15 minutes to dry in Helmand takes 30-40 in Kandahar.

[Letter Home: September 5th]

Parents

If KAF demonstrates the best a multilateral effort can offer, it also provides amus-ing dichotomy of the graft and waste typical of modern welfare. The amount of unnec-essary infrastructure in place to amuse the troops is unreal.

Shall I start with the Canadian hockey rink or the 5,000 square foot game/recreation/media center? It's a roller hockey rink, not an ice hockey rink, though nothing would surprise me. Goals, equipment and other infrastructure has to be pushing half a million dollars, if you consider the cost of delivering stuff here. I find it hilari-ous that, to avoid injury, the Canadians aren't allowed to skate, so they scramble about like its field hockey. Surrounding the hockey rink is the "boardwalk," which is a square-shaped, elevated, and shaded platform bordered by shops and restaurants. One can eat while enjoying a game of hockey or watching the air force girls walking in circles on an asphalt track that appears to be about 1/3 of a mile long.

The wasted funds start at the basic amusement level and go from there. Consider my job at ~$200,000. I don't know exactly how many linguists work here, but I think some safe estimates would indicate ~500-1,000 not counting local national linguists, so we can assume, at a minimum, $100 - $200 million for linguist support alone. Add to that the security contractors, the engineers, and other things and what have we spent. Of course the greatest travesty is that, of the $400 billion allegedly "spent" on the war, so much of it goes directly into the pocket of a contractor, so it's not actually spent on Afghanistan, in a sense that American dollars are leaving American hands. We are just taking it out of one pocket and putting it in another. Has it always been this way? By my tally, the money is equivalent to $15,000 per Afghan in this country, but most of it never leaves American hands.

Why is it that I'm allowed to make $200,000 when an E-3 in the Army can do the same job for $20,000? How does this make sense? In so many cases, we should be drafting non-citizens who are either Afghan or Iranian and forcing them to serve. Got a Green Card? Sign up or get out. America has opened its doors to millions, and just like the Irishmen who stepped off the boat right into the middle of the Civil War; sometimes the piper must be paid. Of course there will always be a need for some civilians, but the proportion of civilian to active duty military is a sham.

Of course, not everyone can wear an American uniform, but for all the Afghan engineers, doctors, lawyers, and scholars who have been living under asylum for twenty years without citizenship, your country needs you.

I have no delusion that an Afghan doctor out of practice for twenty years is in on par with what a modern country has to offer, but they are more advanced than the average Afghan dirt farmer. I envision a Peace Corps expeditionary unit that would take educated, capable people and send them into the fray of whatever nation-building campaign we get involved in.

I'm not making an opinion one way or another on whether we should be involved in nation building, but if that's what the American people want, they deserve more for their money.

Steve

September 7th
Now that I've made it to BAF, I'm taking care of a modest amount of paperwork that needs to be done before my transfer, but in reality this is something of a mini vacation. Between the missed connections and typical travel time, I'm getting nearly a week off. It's a time to enjoy open roads for running

and a selection of books I haven't picked through already. Unfortunately, I know no one here and I miss work and students. The grass is always greener.

September 8th

I'm enjoying a few days of fresh fruit and vegetables here in Bagram. People complain about the food, but on a major installation, it's amazing.

Breakfast options include but are not limited to the following:

Bacon, Canadian bacon, pork sausage, turkey sausage, breakfast burritos, scrambled eggs, hand-made omelets, biscuits and gravy, egg sandwiches, cantaloupe, honey-dew melon, watermelon, pineapple, lettuce, bell peppers, quiche, cobbler, yogurt, as-sorted nuts, rice, and soup

Beverages at any given time include:

Water, Pepsi, Coke, root beer, orange soda, strawberry soda, grape soda, sprite, Dr. Pepper, Diet Pepsi, milk, chocolate milk, banana milk, vanilla soy milk, chocolate soy milk, strong coffee, weak coffee, fruit punch, sweet tea, and unsweetened tea.

Lunch included the following choices:

Roast turkey, assorted lunchmeats, cookies, roast beef, chopped chicken, chili con carne, and corned beef. I won't list the other stuff which is redundant to the morning list of fruits, veggies, drinks, etc.

Supper is a similar collection with additional desserts.

That's not a complete list, but it's what I saw passing through on the way to my table over the course of one day.

On the FOBs it's different, but on the main bases, people are spoiled.

September 9th

I find myself filled with contempt for linguists who complain about their working conditions. The guy next to me on the bus has been complaining for two days about being transferred to Helmand from some place up north. As he griped continuously about our parent company, the military, and every other conceivable entity, I smacked him across the back of the head and told him to be quiet.

September 10th

I decided to have one night of class for my original class of students since I was passing back through Camp Bastion. I'm disappointed that Najibullah has not kept up his speaking ability. However, when he gave me back my dictionary he showed me the pages where he copied the entire dictionary with the Dari and English equivalents. I was blown away by that effort. Class consisted of catching up and reminiscing and involved little to no actual teaching.

[Letter Home: September 10th]

Dear Sheryl,

In regards to your concerns about security risks, simply being here is a security risk, but one of the tenets of the modern American military is risk management rather than risk aversion. I won't speak about all places, but where I was, the two cooks were of the Hazara ethnic group. They love Americans and hate the Taliban as a rule. The Taliban were responsible for some ethnic cleansing that killed somewhere between 2,000 and 10,000 Hazara. Even the Hazara that don't like us because we aren't Muslim, still figure we are better than the Taliban coming back. The other workers were Pashtun, but they were Pashtun from another area, so it is less likely they are going to have a regional grudge that would involve hurting Americans on the base. Finally, some type of background check is done on these guys, and previous workers who have moved on, usually recommend them. As a part of nation building, we prepare the people to manage themselves. So, if we hire a Pashtun and teach him how to use a forklift, that's a Pashtun that knows how to operate a forklift. Now he can be gainfully employed. That's also an American that doesn't need to be deployed or can be freed up to do some fighting instead of driving a forklift all day.

You made a good point regarding old laws still on the books, but I would point out that before we jump to conclusions on the conditions in Afghanistan, we should remember our own history and know that even 30 years ago, we had no problem sending off our daughters into marriage in their early teens. That cultural relativity brings me back to the bacha bazi, which we have discussed. It is illegal, but rule of law in Afghanistan is incredibly lacking, and there are far more important things to worry about. It's usually orphaned boys who are adopted in this manner, bacha bazi or starvation? Starving to death is a legitimate threat. The life expectancy is under forty-five, so from a practical level, I'd have to defend bacha bazi as being a possible re-course to a worse fate. There is a dichotomy of looking down on it at the same time tol-erating it. Because it is the rich and influential people who are doing it, and because there is still so much corruption, it's really not a fight anyone is looking to make. As I said, there are more important things to worry about than a handful of abused or-phans.

Thanks for the mouthwatering image of good running trails. I'll start doing track workouts so I can keep up with you.

Steve

September 11th

Will we forever memorialize those who died on 9/11? Aside from the firefighters and cops who willingly entered a dying building to save people, those that died in were simply in the wrong place at the wrong time—bad luck equivalent to one month of auto fatalities. Even here, we are bombarded with the commentary on that day. However, 10 years after the fact, politicians can't pull us out of here fast enough. Constancy would be nice.

Our transport went through Mirmandab, and I'll be stuck for a couple days. Mia and the medical personnel took my spot on the convoy.

On a lighter note, the whole camp enjoyed volleyball together. The Americans took the series 3-2, but the Afghans held their own including dominating the Ameri-cans 21-6 drubbing in game 2.

I met my Mirmandab Replacement, a Tajik who barely speaks Pashto. Asad openly lamented the ineptitude of my replacement and I am worried about what I'm leaving behind.

[Letter Home: September 11th]

Dear Sheryl,

I've read [*The Kite Runner*]. It's a fun story, but there are a lot of small inaccuracies that make me doubt the veracity of its content. For example, pomegranates don't grow in Kabul. I know that is not a big deal in the grand scheme of things, but lack of attention to detail calls into question the entire plot. I know it's classified as fiction, but the background story isn't, so how do I know trust the history when the story is so poorly woven?

The current year on the Muslim calendar is 1432, and the calendar starts when the prophet Muhammed fled from Mecca to Medina. It's more complicated than that though. In addition to the Gregorian calendar having a 622 year head start on Islam, Muslims use a lunar system, which is several days shorter, so they lose one year against our calendar every ~30 years.

Wow ... your questions are so diverse and complicated. Arab refers to the Se-mitic people in Southern Iraq, going down the Arabic peninsula and across North Af-rica. It also includes a majority of Jews living in Israel, though I'm sure there are plenty of people who would reject that notion out of ignorance. On a side note, I think it's humorous when Fox refers to anti-Semitic Arabs ... Anyway, most Arabs are Mus-lim, but there are considerable Christian populations in Egypt, Lebanon, and Syria with a lot of other pockets of Christianity in Israel, Iraq, and North Africa. Arabs are in the Arabic peninsula, Iraq, and the northern third of Africa. This gets tricky on the self-identification of ethnicity. Sudanese consider themselves Arabic, but they are by American standards, "black." Islam is the religion, and those that practice it are called Muslims. "Islamic" is an adjective, so you might find it thrown in front of things like Islamic world, Islamic people, but the people are still Muslims. The Middle East gener-ally refers to Iran, Iraq, the Arabian Peninsula, and Turkey. You've already identified Persian, which is Iran. It is a distinct ethnic group and language, and they are also Shia Muslim, which is a different sect from the majority of the Islamic world, which is Sunni. Turks are also not Arabic. Sometimes Turkey is referred to as Asia Minor, but who is quibbling? The only Middle Eastern country where the majority is not Muslim is Israel, though Christians make up about 40% of Lebanon. As I mentioned Iranians are Shia. From the outside, there is no difference between Shia and Sunni, but they perceive ancient slights to be of considerable importance, and perception rather than reality is what rules politics in the region.

A new term is Middle East North Africa (MENA), which helps bridge the geo-graphic and intellectual gap of the Arab-Islamic World and the geographic realities that North Africa is obviously south of Europe.

While I have already demonstrated that not all Muslims live in the Middle East, I will point out that the most populous Muslim countries are also not in the Middle East. Indonesia has 200 million, Pakistan 175 million, India 160 million, and Bangla-desh 145 million. I'd also point out that Iran and Turkey, which are non-Arabic, both have 70 million. Egypt is the only Arabic country topping 50 million people. Finally, interestingly enough, China has 20 million. Obviously India has a minority Muslim population, but its overall population is so massive that it leaves India's Muslim popu-lation as the third largest overall. Despite all the disparate cultures and regions in the Islamic world, Saudi Arabia is the spiritual home of Islam and remains ever-important despite it being a small minority of the total Islamic World.

I hope I answered your question. It was very complicated.

Love,

Steve

September 12th

Since I'm stuck here for an undetermined time, I've decided to resume classes, and I went through some basic literacy exercises with Finger's brother-in-law. I have not dealt with a more frustrating person, and at every turn he complains that he does not know anything. I am barely able to control my temper and remark to myself, "no shit! That's why I'm teaching you." I have never had this type of behavior from Afghans before. He's really testing my theory that there are no bad students: only teachers who fail to relate. I'll be out of here soon, so I'm not too worried about it.

Mohammad has returned from his leave in Herat and now Asad Ali has departed. I have my favorite student back and I am pushing him hard over the next few days with constant conversation practice when he's not at work.

September 13th

Well, the long-term ramifications of Ramadan are here. After a month of every Muslim taking half a dozen showers a day for prayer, the well has gone dry. I learned that I could wash my feet, chest, groin, and armpits with 1.5 liters of water. I could have gotten my hair and back with another 1.5 liters. I can't help but chuckle to myself and think that if I'm ever homeless, I'll be in good shape for hygiene. With shorter hair and no beard, I could cut my water usage even further.

September 14th

I taught Mohammad the root word independent, and he's marching around the kitchen using all his words over and over again. Independent; independence, independently, etc. This is so awesome.

September 15th

I'm going crazy from sitting around; I want to go to work.

September 16th

It's an odd sensation to be shivering at 84 Fahrenheit, but I am. The days have been staying in the low hundreds, and with a 30-degree plunge in a matter of hours, the body can't adapt quickly enough, and one feels cold even though it's far warmer than the average centrally cooled house stateside.

They did a number of controlled detonations yesterday; I've been jumpy all morning. I hate that I can't get used to them

September 17th

I'm finally at FOB Robinson, FOB Rob for short; it's named for SFC Christopher L. Robinson who died nearby in 2006 from small arms fire.

September 18th

I got the Army medic to cut a small lipoma out of my back. He was excited at a chance to do something moderately interesting. In the US, it would have cost me $500 for the procedure, a consult, and an initial visit with my primary care doctor in order to get the consult. Here, it took one swab of alcohol, a dab of lidocaine, a slice with a scalpel, and three stitches for a procedure that took less than 10 minutes.

September 19th

FOB Rob is up on top of a hill, and I can get a taste of impending winter from the gusts of wind that whirl their way up here.

It's odd to be around women for the first time in months; Mia is living two doors down from me. There are also two Air Force nurses, one of whom gives me a warm smile that I can only assume I'm misreading.

There are some other old faces are here as well. Dave and Sayed, my old coworkers are here and I'm looking forward to working with them again.

I taught class tonight. There are several Uzbeks and Turkmen, which are ethnic groups I've never dealt with. One of them didn't even know Dari, so I had to say something in Dari and wait for his cousin to translate it from Dari to Uzbek. I don't expect him to stay in the class with such a difficult language barrier. I also have a soldier, a mechanic, and a few other workers that are attending class for now. Three are brothers: Daoud, Saleem, and Fazal Saleem. The fourth is Ali, unrelated to the Ali brothers in Mirmandab; he's an older gentleman with an obvious addiction to opium who shows up with red eyes to every event. He insists that he is just tired, but everyone knows better. I am very optimistic about working with him, because he told me he wants to learn English to help his grandchildren. I'm ecstatic that he would want to learn from me and pass it on to his kids. Things like that make me have less doubts about what we do here. It give me hope for the future. Islam is one other student who works in the kitchen—an incredibly shy Uzbek that has difficulty expressing himself around the Pashtuns. I suspect I will need to segregate classes for him. This is a common occurrence, some of the minority groups to be uncomfortable under the perceived watchful eye of the majority ethnic group. The Pashtuns have been at the head of the lion's share of atrocities in this country, and the distrust is often palpable.

September 20th

I had a laugh tonight when my student said, "I'm a cook; I work in the chicken."

The Taliban have assassinated Former President Rabbani. He was the "peace envoy" of the Afghan government that was responsible for negotiating with the insurgents. Some are calling this an example of what negotiating with the Taliban means; others are saying he was just another warlord and good riddance.

I think I tend to side with the latter. I think we are at a point where Afghanistan is better off without the old guard, and while the government does need to settle things with the Taliban, they need someone from the new era, not another speen giri (white beard) who helped cause the creation of the Taliban to begin with.

[Letter Home: September 20th]

Dad,

Perfunctory Salutations,

I wanted to clarify a point in my last letter. I said we've spent ~$15,000 per Af-

ghan, but the point was that most of the money we've spent has gone into our own pockets. $15,000 per Afghan would mean essentially doubling or tripling the annual household income of Afghanistan for every year of occupation. While, of course, having a sudden influx of money is not always economically sound, but it would allow an ability to not only import foreign goods and create the capital for small business development.

Instead, our expenditures have circled inside our own economy and so little actually reaches the target.

We can't go a week without an article about corruption in Kabul, but I think Western journalists or perhaps Western citizens have failed miserably if they think $500 billion has been spent on this war without rampant corruption stateside. I think it's expected that a third-world shithole is to have its share of corruption, but how much corruption goes on with campaigns that are financed by defense contract kickbacks?

Maybe I'm off on a tangent, but the cost of everything we've done is unreal, and we deserve more for our money as taxpayers.

Steve

September 21st

I have internet in my room. It's the little things that make me happy.

I got a real haircut today for the first time in ages. The Arabs have a barber from Kabul who is quite skilled at what he does and his English is decent. I feel refreshed and less like an animal. The barber is typical of the affluence that has increased with the creation of a middle class in Afghanistan. While most of the country is immeasurably poor, those that have gone to the city and learned technical skills have nowhere to go but up. While private or public donors often pay for these schools, eventually they will become self-sufficient.

The opulence of our Arab partners is amazing. Only they would have an Astroturf soccer field.

The section that is officially FOB Rob is approximately the same size as VSP Mirmandab, but there is a safe area around outside the gate that allows a decent run along the inside of the perimeter.

The facilities of FOB Rob are much better than Mirmandab, and it's a testament to the enduring presence in this facility that has been open for nearly six years. The number of Afghan workers working on the facilities is more than ten, with three working in the laundry facility, three working in the chow hall, one mechanic, and a handful of others responsible for various tasks such as trash removal. This is not including a few Indian and Kenyan workers who are responsible for cleaning the bathrooms and maintaining the generators.

The chow hall is a hardened facility with a big screen TV and air-conditioning, and the kitchen is quite large, boasting deep fryers, multiple grills, and several refrigerators for storage. There is a sizable contingent of Marines here, but I won't report precise numbers. Residences mostly consist of shipping containers, but there are a few B-huts as the numbers of personnel here have grown over the last year. There are over a dozen American contractors of various types. Our gym is also a hardened facility, but it is on a slant, and the poorly routed power results in the three treadmills shorting out after anywhere from 5 to 15 minutes. There are two elliptical machines and four mechanical stationary bikes, two 'total gyms,' and medicine balls along with the standard free weights one would expect in any gym. The Afghan soldiers are allowed to use the gym and the chow hall, and some of the Americans have worked with the Afghans to improve their overall fitness.

There is a gate guarded by Afghan security guards, and outside that is a HESCO perimeter that allows for a continuous run of 15-25 minutes depending on pace. Along the southern edge of this is a shooting range, a helicopter pad, and an adobe compound that houses the Afghan security guards. Nearby, the Arab compound provides another round of running that can be supplemented by the relatively soft ground underneath the soccer field. There is a clinic down the hill from all of this that holds free clinics and lessons for women who are bold enough to show up.

September 22nd

I've decided to teach only five days a week giving myself the night off for both Thursday and Friday.

Afsir is an interesting student. He is a Captain who started off as an enlisted soldier and he's been in for seven years. He understands English, having heard it constantly for years, but he has difficulty expressing himself. Rahman is a mechanic who speaks well, but he can't read and write. He is ethnically Pashtun, but he looks Hispanic, and most people assume he's a western contractor. Sergeant Major Khan, who I've met and talked to on several occasions is stationed here, and I'm very excited to work with him.

September 24th

Dave has another pet in addition to his dog Colby. It's a cross-eyed red tabby. It makes itself at home in my room when Dave is at work, but I am sure it's completely retarded. Dave just calls it "cat." Mia calls it "Pisho," which is Pashto for cat.

September 25th

Afghans employed by KBSS do base security, but an American security contractor named Charlie leads them. He is a mountain of a man, standing well over a head taller than me, and he ripples with muscles that dwarf the AK-47 he carries. He's an ex-marine covered in tattoos related to patriotism and the corps. One could trace his career by his tattoos. Rozi, is a Dari-Turkmen interpreter, but he also speaks some English, so I asked Charlie if Rozi should come to class; Charlie is going to make English a daily requirement for Rozi.

Islam the cook is coming along nicely in pronunciation, but I think he lacks comprehension. At least he's trying. Rahman and Afsir both ask a lot of good questions. Rahman has been working with the Americans for eight years, and his comprehension is fantastic. However, his grammar is non-existent, and he's barely literate in either language. I'm hoping that I can form an advanced class with him in order to hone some of his better skills and enhance his weaknesses.

Ali's age and addiction interferes with his retention, but I will double my efforts with him.

September 26th

They had pizza in the chow hall today. It was as good as anything stateside, and as a result I'm in an absurdly good mood.

Afsir ate lunch with me. One of his soldiers was shot in the face and has some eye damage. He'll get medical treatment at KAF then some time with family before coming back.

September 28th

SPC James A. Butz, Marine SGT Nicholas A. Sprovtsoff, and Marine SGT Christopher Diaz died today. They were all good guys. Billy, the corpsman was severely wounded. I've been told it's his third purple heart. I knew these three men as Butz, EOD Nick, and Chris the dog handler. They will be missed.

There isn't anything else to say about that.

September 29th

I feel guilty about my relief that Alba survived. The last thing I said to him yesterday before he left on a convoy back to Mirmandab was a half-assed, "keep your head down," and a commitment to have a drink with him stateside.

I feel utterly drained.

September 30th

These deaths will push deaths over fifty for the month of September.

All I can say is that I am glad to have worked with these guys. I believe in what we have done here, and I don't feel they have died in vain. I know that this type of thing is likely little comfort for their survivors, but without grandstanding or demeaning their worth, I hope that America is aware of their sacrifice and understands the debts we owe all of the people who have died here.

6

OCTOBER-NOVEMBER

October 1st

The replacement for SGT Diaz is here for a couple days until he catches a ride to Mirmandab. I wonder what goes through his head as he prepares to replace someone who died. They probably knew each other, in such a small community.

October 2nd

I'm caught up on my reading.

Every FOB has a makeshift library. People send books in the mail, guys pick up books at bigger installations, and guys bring books from home.

The bigger installations really have a nice selection. Bagram has over 1,000 volumes in the MWR I frequent, and I've never really looked at the other MWR, but I know it's just as big.

October 3rd

Class is going very well. Rahman and Islam have become class leaders. I'm gradually refining my methods, now that I have more experience with this. I have developed what I'm calling a 5 X 4 method for vocabulary retention. While a child needs to only hear a new word a few times for it to stick, adults need much more repetition. I am telling my students that they need to read a word five times, write a word five times, hear a word five times, and say a word five times for them to retain it. Of course some words come more easily than others and the method is not foolproof, but it seems to be the average time for retention.

There was a memorial service yesterday in Mirmandab for Nick, Chris, and Butz. Evidently the EOD guys wired the podium to blow up after the service was over as a tribute to the EOD services of Nick. I wish I could have been there. I'm proud of their sacrifice.

EOD Nick was doing routine disposal of an IED when something went wrong. While it was possibly human error, Nick has as much time defusing these things as anyone in the country, so I suspect it was something more complicated than any of us will ever actually know. Nick survived the initial blast with his legs and right arm blown off; Billy and Chris retrieved him and were carrying his body clear of the area. Butz, ran across open ground in order to assist Billy, who would be responsible for put-ting three tourniquets on Nick, in addition to dealing with multiple superficial wounds which are a tremendous source of infection secondary to the initial wounds. A second IED went off while they were moving Nick. Chris's body was hurled over nearby HES-COs, Butz was blown backwards, and Nick's body cushioned the blast to protect Billy. The bodies could not be recovered that day. With an unknown number of IEDs in the area and the nearest EOD tech dead, they would have to wait until the next day when EOD techs from elsewhere arrived for clearance. Multiple Marines and soldiers were left in a nearby bunker to protect the bodies from marauding dogs and rats. Over the course of the evening vigilant marksmanship kept three dogs and over a dozen rats from desecrating the bodies any further.

October 4th

Mark is back to calling me John Walker Lindh, though he acknowledges that I looked slightly less like John Walker Lindh since the haircut. He asks me about my terrorist plots and I feign irritation and tell him that he keeps interrupting me while I am developing my ideas so I can't commit terrorism.

Dave is leaving soon; he's completed his tour and is going home.

October 6th

I met two local national linguists who are terrified to lose their jobs last night. A Taliban prisoner called them "slaves to America and traitors to Islam," so they punched him. I can't remember either of their names, but one was truly at his wits end.

"I can't go back to Jalalabad. The Taliban have my picture, and they'll kill me." He said that he'd be tortured if they captured him, so he might as well kill him-self; I have no idea if he's exaggerating. There is no doubt that they'd find out where his family lives and kill and torture them too. That's not an exaggeration.

In 2009, two local national linguists had their faces cut off. I don't mean be-headed; I mean their faces were cut off. It staggers the mind to imagine precisely what happens when one's face is cut off. Thank god they both died of shock shortly thereafter.

I am frustrated at those back home that criticize us for mistakes that result in un-wanted or unnecessary death, but those aren't intentional. There is a big difference be-tween accidents and deliberate acts of mayhem with no particular target. Motorcycle bombs in crowded market places with no coalition forces for miles are commonplace.

October 7th

When someone departs, they often leave a treasure trove of unopened hygiene products, clothes, and other tidbits rather than take them home. Rooms are plundered within hours of departure, and I believe I got to Dave's room first, given that his stash of porn was still intact. Unfortunately it is the same stack of old Playboys I read at Camp Bastion that have remained in circulation. There is no sign of *Bangin' Mommy*.

Today in the chow hall, I had an interesting conversation with Mark about adultery. We were discussing women who get lonely when their men are overseas. "I don't think adultery is right, but Jesus forgave, so I think given the circumstances I'd have to do the same."

Some are more callous about it. Gunny Mick in Mirmandab said that he assumed his wife was fooling around when he was gone, and he called her three days be-fore returning to make sure she had removed any blatant evidence of infidelity.

This isn't to say that all women fool around; most probably don't, but enough do that anyone with a strong sense of self-survival doesn't have blinders on to the possibil-ity, and they don't look too closely for evidence when they get back.

I can't blame a lonely wife for wanting some companionship after several months.

October 8th

Today, I got another haircut from the Tajik barber. The Arab in front of me got a shave with a straight razor, but he was cut up pretty good, so I declined the straight razor shave and just went with a buzzer on the lower edges of my beard.

I work with the Afghans, and I trust the ones I work with, but I think it's asking a lot to let a strange man, Afghan or not, place a razor against my throat.

I introduced the two local national interpreters to Charlie yesterday, and he's looking into getting them new jobs with the security company. He said there is no reason for good interpreters to be wasted because they punched a Talib.

October 9th

Most of my students are taking leave. Rahman and Rozi are all I have left, so I am going forward with changing my format to include more diversification when everyone has returned. These two students will be so far ahead of everyone else that they need their own class.

The two interpreters were falling over themselves to give me gifts after I helped them. I tried to say I hadn't done much, but they insisted. They gave me a bunch of trinkets, some sandals, and a nice Shalwar Kamis (man dress). It's a heck of a souvenir, even if I don't have a place to wear it.

October 10th

Today is the first prolonged rain I've seen in Helmand. There were periodic showers in the summer, but this was a major weather system. It drizzled and poured off-and-on for the entire day. The air is distinctly cold now, and I think it's safe to say winter is almost here. I'll need to buy a few pants when I go on leave, because it will only get worse.

Getting closer to my departure, I shaved the beard and left the moustache as a joke. It is the most absurd 1970's "pornstache," and I'm rocking the hell out of it. Mark almost fell down in laughing

October 11th

I think the Taliban probed the base defenses last night. I'm not sure. It didn't sound like the usual random gunshots. It appears that we'll be under 600 deaths for the year, maybe even be under 550. That's a lot less than last year's total of 708.

October 12th

"Cat" died today. He crawled into one of the big AC units and electrocuted himself. I'm wondering if one of the Afghan soldiers put him in there as a joke and it went bad.

There was always something weird about that cat, and I don't think it's a big loss. October 13th

I haven't been working the last couple days, but I'm almost out of here. I catch a convoy tomorrow, and I'm getting the fuck out of here for a few weeks. I'm considering a marathon on the way out of here, but I haven't made up my mind.

October 15th

Dave is still in transit to BAF and his final departure from Afghanistan. He managed to lose Colby (his dog), which means she was probably shot. He had already arranged for her to get transportation back to the US. Including vaccinations and transport, it costs $3,000 to bring a dog back from Afghanistan.

October 18th

I'm out of here. I didn't bother with the marathon because my shoes are getting too worn down. I'll order some to arrive while I'm stateside and push for the marathon on my way back.

I got a great look at the Kariz system on the flight from Helmand to KAF. I'm on the plane out of the country from KAF to Dubai and then on through England to San Diego. They gave us two beers each. I'm drunk off two.

[Three weeks of leave stateside]

November 10th

I'm back.

From waking up in San Diego to falling asleep in Afghanistan, I was up for just under 48 hours. I managed a bit of fitful sleep in London and on the jet, but it wasn't particularly restful.

The weather has changed significantly since I left. The nights slip into the 40s and 50s, and we expect freezing soon. The winter monsoons will be kicking off as well. It is an interesting climate going from 120 degrees and bone dry in the summer to freezing and torrential rain in the winter.

I've taken up a new hobby given that I cannot safely bird watch. I've taken to learning constellations. So far, I've added Pleiades and Taurus. A rather aggressive goal is one new constellation a week. I'll need time, clear skies, and ideally, a cooperative moon. As much time as I've spent staring up at them, it's a pity I don't know more constellations.

November 11th

I did a marathon on Veteran's Day. I can't say it was a Veteran's Day Marathon, because it was the marathon I planned on doing before leave, but the timing was nice regardless. I got up at 0200 and ran around for 4:01:00. I didn't have a precise way to measure the run, so I figured that 4 hours would be long enough. I meandered all over Leatherneck and Bastion including a trip out to the far side of the flight line and back. I've never gone to the Italian section before, and it would be nice to check out their little pizzeria that's next to their chow hall.

November 12th

I'm back at FOB Robinson; I lost my old room and the new room is absolute shit. My old room is reserved for "VIPs," but VIPs don't spend the night at FOB Rob. It took me all day to track down the stuff I left in my room, haphazardly packed up by some of the Marines.

November 15th

I've gotten settled in to my work schedule.

Charlie has quit his job doing base security in exchange for something a little more hands-on. Bob is his replacement, and he's a very personable guy with similar attitudes to me. We have a shared disillusionment with the day-to-day grind stateside. We go home, and we see the exact same people doing the exact same thing right where we left them 5, 10, 20 years ago. We commiserated about those that need constant help from outside sources, but fail to lift a finger on their own behalf. He was very angry when he said we've been so prosperous for so long, that we've forgotten to think on our feet.

He's been over here since the beginning of the war after he departed the military. He is married and still has US citizenship, but for tax purposes, he's an ex-pat, and he's only home in the US for two weeks out of the year, if he chooses to go home at all.

[Letter Home: November 15th]

Dear Andrea,

I officially "graduated" today. I'm not sure what's entailed in graduating from an online master's program; I'm certainly not leaving the internet. Typical of most events in my life, I looked at my watch and thought, "Oh ... I graduated today," before going about my business. I'm mildly disappointed I didn't graduate "with distinction." That arbitrary achievement would have enhanced the validity of my degree in a world where online programs are still stigmatized, albeit, some correctly so. I'm not sure if I'll use my degree actively or if it will be just another tool in the toolbox like journalism and languages.

I'm still upset the [International Relations] department rejected my thesis proposal, which, though very in depth and complicated, mostly centered on fornicating with as many foreign women as I could. The program director said I was missing the point of International Relations; I replied that HE was missing the point of International Relations.

I believe world peace is possible, and I will pursue that dream, one irresponsible dalliance at a time. I can say, "May I sleep with your sister?" in five languages.

Historically, the spoils of war included women, so let us dispense with the war and get to the shagging. It's not the first time I've been called a man ahead of my time.

As with most phases of my life, I think to myself, "What now?" Perhaps if my motivation were ever more than thinking something is a good idea at the time, I would have an answer for "What now?" but as it stands, I'm doomed to sink into a bout of self-loathing and depression exacerbated by angry masturbation and crying into my pillow ...

Perhaps I should pursue my thesis ideas independently of the university.

My next goal is making wine in Afghanistan. It seemed like a good idea at the time.

Steve

November 16th

I went down to the Afghan Security Group (ASG) compound and met their commander. The whole group is Turkmen including my student Rozi. I had a late lunch in the Commander's quarters consisting of lamb and rice for the main meal then almonds, green raisins, soy beans, candied pistachios, and Turkmen bread.

The Turkmen bread is typical flat bread that I'm used to in this part of the world, but what made it unique was that they baked small pieces of sheep fat into the dough, so as one chews, there are little bursts of tasty grease in the crust. The texture took some time to get used to, but the taste was fantastic.

I'll admit I had indigestion.

I've added an Afghan major and a sergeant to my students.

The Afghan major is going to be tough, because he demands extra attention beyond what a regular class will give him. In America, there is still a subtle divide between officers and enlisted, but in the third world that divide is stark in a place where corporal punishment still exists and authority is wielded with impunity. I have no use for his sense of entitlement and social status, and while I will do one-on-one lessons with the Major in the short term, once he is ready, I'll be dumping him in with the rest of the students.

The sergeant, Ishaq is bold, opinionated, and a lot of fun. He also has a broad vocabulary and picks up things quickly. The other night, he provided a moment of laughter for everyone when his Jalalabad dialect mixed up the P with an F and he called the neighboring country Fakistan instead of Pakistan. The conversation quickly digressed into chants of "Fuck Pakistan!"

I laughed till it hurt; I'm accomplishing something, even if I don't know what.

November 17th

I've been moved to a night shift. I've just gotten into a rhythm of sleeping 8 hours without the use of Nyquil or Tylenol PM. So it goes.

Mission first, so I won't even chronicle the irritation I feel. An old guy is coming, and it's harder on an older person to flip-flop by 12 hours than it is on me, so I'll take that for the team. I suspect I'm going to get sick though; I've just gotten used to the dust and the cold weather and gotten on a reasonable sleep cycle, so I imagine that switching by 12 hours will push my immune system over the edge.

I got a bunch of mail that was forwarded to me from my old location. It had been shoved in a drawer somewhere, and I finally got ahold of it.

I've made the same mistake of overestimating the abilities of some of my weaker students. It's frustrating that I've wasted their time. I'm going to subdivide the classes because I've just found out that the brothers can't read and write. Of course, if they hadn't lied to me initially, I could have done things differently, but so it goes.

[Letter Home: November 17th]

Dad,

Thanks for the note, the articles, and the [Reader's Digest] writing submission card. Mail wasn't being forwarded properly, so I've just gotten a backlog of about two-months' worth of mail. I have not had time to read the articles but I shall get to them shortly. Given the late receipt of my mail, the deadline for Reader's Digest is long past, but I am preparing a short piece for wildlife magazines regarding birding in a combat zone.

Along with my mail, I received my *Birds of the Indian Subcontinent*. I'm still moderately enthusiastic about creating a *Birds of Afghanistan*. I had a decent idea recently of going to American zoos to shoot photographs of whatever relevant species I can find. Not having to pay for use or contact owners of photos would certainly cut down on time and production costs.

Speaking of bird photography, while I was on leave, I bought a 55-200mm lens for my Nikon, because the 18-55mm just wasn't doing the job.

As I told you previously, I'm pursuing some beginner's astronomy by learning new constellations. Afghanistan is a great place for it, given the sparsely populated areas and nonexistent power grids. Last night, I learned Cassiopeia. I think I spelled that right. I fear my spelling, already atrocious, will be even worse as I try to document Greek and Roman mythology traipsing across the midnight sky.

So far, I know Big Dipper, North Star, Orion's Belt, Taurus, Cassiopeia, and Pleiades. At one per week, I'll have nearly 60 constellations and other prominent celestial bodies within a year. Of course, some things I "know" but I don't really know such as Mars and Venus; some things I've always known like the first three in the previous list. Perhaps I'm merely trainspotting, but I can't imagine that stargazing is any worse than my other manic pursuits. It's certainly far less destructive.

I've been moved to the night shift, which is fine by me. I'd hate to waste daylight on my work, which is important but mind numbing. A 2200-0600 shift will work out well. The only problem is that I've been in country for over a week now, and I've slipped into a good sleep cycle. Now of course, I'll have to flip that upside down. Tylenol PM will help get me back on track but I use it reluctantly out of fear of addiction to sleeping pills in general. I never allow myself to use anything like that for more than two nights in a row. I'd hate to end up like Elvis.

Steve

PS: I was referring to Elvis succumbing to addiction and dying from heart attack while on the john. Viva Las Vegas was pretty awful too, so I didn't want there to be any confusion.

November 18th

I'm on the new schedule now. Stimulants and downers will be part of my diet—oh well.

I have half a bottle of Hydroxycut and half a bottle of Tylenol PM. Neither of those are going to last to the end of this deployment, but I'll ration them as well as I can. I actually won't use the Hydroxycut for more than a few days, because it's hell on my kidneys. I never use the Tylenol PM for more than 2 days straight out of fear of creating a habit from the stuff.

I've yet to organize my stuff from being moved to the new room, and the mess is depressing.

I had a great feeling today, when I found Rozi helping a Turkmen laborer understand the letters of Dari. For all intents and purposes, the nearly one million Turkmen in Afghanistan do not use an alphabet for their own language, and those who wish to be literate must learn to read and write in Dari. Rozi has been helping some of his fellow Turkmen understand the alphabet. The typical Afghan has an unhealthy competitive spirit; there is so little to

Poppy harvesting

have here that they will sabotage a fellow countryman, just to keep a little sliver of the pie. This isn't the case with Rozi, who is ambitious, but not to the detriment of those around him.

That's the impact I want to have on this country. I want to train the trainers, so that eventually our role here will be limited to nonexistent. These people are so eager to learn and so eager for a better life. If Rozi can teach someone else after learning to teach from me, I'll have done something that will stay behind after I've left.

November 19th

I just got finished teaching for 2 hours and I'm tired.

My three illiterate students have dwindled to two; one has gone on leave. I'm still working on basic literacy. I have three advanced English students and we are going over more complicated issues. There's a new addition who is at an intermediate level, with lots of canned phrases but little vocabulary.

November 20th

Yesterday the ANA and Marines went to Kajaki, and while there, they went fishing. The Major was gutting fish when he got back and missed class. Fazli helped him clean the fish, and he must have gotten fish guts on his clothing, because the stench was overpowering.

He and his two brothers are usually dirty, but I can tolerate it. This is only the second time in Afghanistan that a lack of hygiene has made me nearly gag.

Ahmad hasn't been coming to literacy class, and I suspect he has given up entirely. I gave Fazli three lines of text to copy for homework and went over some words, so that was that.

November 21st

The Major is frustrating me with his dedication to perfect pronunciation. I'm more concerned with fluency and fluidity, and the correct pronunciation will come later. Everyone learns differently, but I'm partial to my method.

Fazal Saleem frustrated me tonight when I caught him trying to cheat on some of the words we've been learning. He doesn't know how to read and write, but he is intelligent enough. I provided a list of words for him to study, but they were too difficult for him. Instead of studying them, he memorized them as literate Afghans read them to him. He was smart enough to remember the words on the page, but his finger would be on word number five while he was reading word number two. If he would put as much effort into learning as he does trying to trick me, he'd be much better off. I told him if he tries to fool me again I will stop teaching him. He appeared extremely apologetic.

I'm dumping the Major in with my main class next week. That will make six regular students.

November 23rd

I'm sick; it's not a surprise. The shift change has caught up with me. I told Will that I'm coming in 2 hours late tonight so I can get a few extra minutes of rest, and I'm going to cancel class for the next two days until I recover. I am usually able to burst through a cold in two days, but the congestion on this one will take longer. The nurse gave me some Cepacol lozenges and some Sudafed. I hate that I'm going to be sick for thanksgiving.

November 24th

Thanksgiving was fantastic, but I ate in my room because I didn't want to blow my nose every 20 seconds in front of people who were trying to eat. The Army cook outdid himself with a fantastic spread that would rival a meal typical stateside.

November 26th

My arrogance has caught up with me. The result of throwing the Major in with the regular class is his complete domination of my time, at the expense of the more senior students who defer to his interruptions. I'll give it another day or two and move the Major back to his own class. I cannot overcome this cultural limitation, so it's better to just keep them separate.

November 30th

Tonight in class, I showed some of my students how to make a rubber-band gun by wrapping the rubber band from the tip of the index finger around the thumb and onto the tip of the pinky finger. They had never seen it before. Friends and family said I could never make a difference here. I have certainly proved them wrong now. [Joking]

The Arabs changed the muezzin for the prayer call*. He sounds like a bag of drowning cats.

*The muezzin is responsible for announcing the prayer time and for reciting the prayer in the mosque. Each day begins and ends with a long rambling in Arabic over the intercom in the Arabic compound nearby.

November ends with coalition deaths under 30; the first time monthly casualties have been under 30 since May of 2009 and the lowest number of casualties for November since 2008.

7

DECEMBER

December 1st

I feel like I'm getting back into a routine since having my schedule turned upside down. I have hopes for this last month of December to stay relatively calm and keep coalition deaths under 30.

[Letter home: December 3rd]

Dear Claude,

December has been quiet so far, and we are entering the third day with no coalition deaths. Barring a string of bad luck, there will be less coalition deaths this December than last December, which, like most months this year, have allowed total casualties to dip below 600. This will still be the second most deadly year in the war, but considering last year's high of 719, I think the numbers show some sort of progress. I get caught up in the numbers a lot, because it's the way I think, but there are many intangi-ble signs of progress as well. The most important is the steadily improving Afghan Na-tional Army. They have been taking on more and more responsibility, and they are truly being tested as a modern military force, and by and large, I think they pass that test.

Of course, the coalition will need a continued presence for some time—special op-erations and air force. The Afghan Air Force is all but non-existent at this point with smattering of Soviet era Aircraft and American trained pilots. I assume some of the European countries have also provided training.

I loathe to think of pulling out troops in an active fight. There can and should be a draw down, but a complete pullout is dangerous. What frustrates me is that no one speaks of the troops we have surrounding China or the leftovers from the Cold War in Western Europe. How many billions have we spent maintaining our buffers against the Soviet Union 20 years after it crumbled? Sure, we need some strategic presence, but in many cases, our presence is a catalyst for dangerous activities. Was Iran actively pursuing a nuclear weapon before we had 30,000 troops within immediate strik-ing distance across the Gulf?

On a lighter note, stargazing has gone well, and I've met an amateur geologist who is helping me learn some of the geologic formations. Afghanistan is one of the most mineral rich countries in the world, and if they could ever exploit that, they would be a very wealthy country. Simply walking around, one comes across hemalite (iron ore) the size of soccer balls, and while hemalite itself is not worth that much, it's indicative of the other things available including lithium deposits that are allegedly worth trillions. China and India are competing to open up mineral exploration, but I worry about how much money is going to stay in the country; even a small percentage would be a boon to a country with a GDP smaller than Warren Buffet's net worth.

I'm hopeful for this place. A little bit of security and some development can make it great.

Bert, the amateur geologist, makes rock gardens from the various formations. I found a place while running that is incredibly diverse with great big chunks of various minerals, and I packed about 60 pounds up with my rucksack. I'm taking him down to that place tomorrow, and I'll bring my rucksack sack to fill up for another load. I'll also start my own rock garden.

Okay, I'll admit that my commentary on rocks is boring, but I'm bored, so sue me.

Steve

December 5th
Sometimes working with Saleem is taking a step back for every two steps forward. He writes well, but I'm confused at his ability to read. I wonder if he's dyslexic, but there is no way to diagnose it. I've been changing my tactics a little bit and breaking things down into syllables, and having him practice sounds over and over again. I'll right ob, bob, cob, dob, fob, etc. in Pashto and then when he has mastered all the consonants and vowels that can proceed the "b" sound, I switch around to ba, bab, bac, bad, baf, etc.. I'm not even worrying about him understanding words. I'll break it down into the simplest concepts and go from there.

December 6th
I'm continually frustrated by many Afghan-Americans who are so lazy and indif-ferent to local Afghans. Only by sheer luck and compassion from America have they been able to be citizens of the United States, but they act as if they are something spe-cial. The difference between a prosperous Afghan-American, and an illiterate farmer in Helmand is a visa.

December 8th
Yesterday was one of the worst events in recent Afghan history. Approximately 55 Shia Muslims were killed in Kabul by a huge blast from a suicide bomber. The Tali-ban have disavowed the attack, and it has been claimed by Lashkar-e-Jhangvi al Almi, a Pakistani terrorist group with allegiances to Al Qaeda.

The good news for long term stability is that the Taliban has, for the most part, refrained from the types of sectarian attacks that ripped apart Iraq for so long. However, as the Taliban claim no responsibility, they have blamed "foreign influences" as being a destabilizing force in Afghanistan. I wonder if they are referring to the US or Pakistan.

December 9th

It seems there have been back-to-back horrific events lately. Today was an accident claimed by the Taliban; a Taliban IED that was meant for a British convoy destroyed a bus.

Why do the Western media fail to cover these events but sensationalize events when Americans or other coalition partners screw up?

The Taliban are responsible for 70 percent of civilian deaths. Often those civilian deaths are deliberate.

I don't suggest that we deserve a free pass, and events should be reported, but it seems that predator journalists scrambling for a byline and a good title are content to attack our own troops rather than report everything with an impartial hand.

December 10th

This is the first morning I haven't heard an IED. I never knew I'd be skittish around explosions, but I think some people are and others aren't. I feel the explosion as much as I hear it. It travels through the earth and vibrates the body. The shockwave causes the generator to skip a beat.

I passed day 200 of my year in country last week, but I didn't even notice or care. I've not ever counted the days, and a major milestone was just another day.

There was an eclipse tonight, and the Afghans were trembling in fear, because it was "a bad omen from God" and "punishment for sin."

[Essay on the Lunar Eclipse]

I could not understand the utter fear caused by the lunar eclipse, and it was the first time in my tour that I can truly attest to culture shock. Poor hygiene, low-to-nonexistent literacy, and many other things I could equate to the poor infrastructure and lack of schooling, but when it came to the reaction to the eclipse, I was astounded. While there is a fundamentalist Christian element to American society, for the most part, I feel that I've been raised in a culture that focuses predominantly on empiricism over superstition. This is decidedly not the case in a country dominated by fundamental interpretations and outright superstition for many events that Westerners shrug off. This includes lunar activity.

When Dod Saleem came to me to discuss the "Bad Sign," at first I didn't even realize what he was talking about. I'd noted the eclipse, chastised myself for not paying better attention to current events, and went on about my evening. He told me that this was a bad omen sent by God to warn people about their sinful ways. All manner of things happened during the time of an eclipse, and he spoke so fast that much of it was lost in translation, but the most poignant part was that families would mourn and pray for salvation on a night like this, and a baby born during an eclipse would need a goat slaughtered on its behalf. Dod Saleem was incredibly nervous, but Ali was shaking in fear. Red-eyed, and nearly in tears, he asked to leave early to go pray. Among all the rest of the Afghans in the chow hall and around the barracks there was an aura of discontent, and I didn't need to interview all of them to make sense of it. Even Rahman half-heartedly assented to the superstitions, but I insisted he come to my class anyway; he wanted to know what I thought, but I needed a white board to properly illustrate my explanation.

While there isn't anything explicitly negative about the eclipse in the Koran, the Old Testament references the negative connotations associated with eclipses, and the Old Testament is an inseparable part of Islamic tradition.

Joel 2:31-32 "The sun shall be turned to darkness, and the moon to blood, before the great and awesome day of the Lord comes. 32 And it shall come to pass that everyone who calls on the name of the Lord shall be saved. For in Mount Zion and in Jerusalem there shall be those who escape, as the Lord has said, and among the survivors shall be those whom the Lord calls."

Amos 8: 9 "'And [in the end],' declares the Lord God, 'I will make the sun go down at noon and darken the earth in broad daylight.'"

Obviously the second verse is referring only to a solar eclipse, but I use it to lead into my next point which is that I think what makes Rozi and Rahman so unique in my experiences here. They both are set apart from the rest of the Afghans with whom I've worked. Hajmal, Mohammad Ali, Najibullah, and others have all been exceptionally smart, but I question if they will ever have the depths of experience to build a bridge between our societies. Rozi is well educated and as far as I can tell is filled with an innate curiosity that transcends the bonds of religion. Rahman, while less educated has worked with the coalition for so long that we have simply rubbed off on him to the point that he trusts us to not lead him astray. He assumes that we have it all figured out. They were the only two who attended my English class the night of the eclipse. Both asked me for my opinion, and after I drew a diagram of celestial bodies on the white board, both seemed to accept the possibility that it was merely the earth blocking the light of the sun. I wasn't trying to convince them. I was just passing off what I believed on the issue, and they felt it made more sense than the superstition they'd been brought up with. For both of them, it was an epiphany.

In societies such as Afghanistan, we cannot take for granted that the country as a whole can be capable of understanding our level of empiricism just as we may not be able to understand their level of superstition. This puts further burden on those who can understand fundamental approaches to religion as well as the complexities of Western science, economics, and politics. Whether they are Americans who have im-

European Starlings

mersed themselves in this culture or Afghans who have worked alongside Americans for years at a time, they have the unique role of developing understanding between two different societies. It's not that I necessarily think that our empiricism is right or that their superstition is wrong. It's that without some basic understanding of both, our worlds cannot coexist.

December 14th

In literacy class, Saleem is finally coming along. He still makes mistakes, but they are less often. I've got a new recruit for this class as well. Islam, a good student from earlier in the fall has come back from leave, but he has fallen behind. He was very shy before when dealing with the raucous Pashtuns, so I have decided to let him help me with Saleem rather than force his participation in the general class.

Some students asked about Christmas today, and I had a hard time explaining parts of it. While Muslims are familiar with the Christ story, other aspects of our culture including Santa Claus, Christmas Trees, and other things sound so silly to someone who has not spent their whole life indoctrinated into the culture. It tested my limits in Pashto to explain the pagan origins of most of our traditions.

Muslims respect Christians as imperfect Muslims, but I was leery of teaching too students who might be offended depending on their religiosity. I felt it would be a good move to build rapport by teaching the Afghans "Merry Christmas," and Americans are initially shocked but then smile when the Afghans greet them. Of course, I'm going to run into trouble if a militant atheist gets offended at being told Merry Christmas. Hopefully no one takes themselves that seriously.

Another week has flashed by; I'm 5 months from completion.

December 16th

They have Christmas decorations up now including a big Santa Claus in the chow hall. I hope my students ask more questions about Christmas, because it will provide a good learning experience for both of us.

I've decided to start a garden in the spring. I can grow a few crops in a 4 X 4 square. I'll order some supplies in January.

I'm also planning on ordering birdseed to attract new species. At this point, I'm just coming up with projects to kill time. December 18th

Three sleeping pills and three hours of sleep; this is a hell of a drug ratio I'm on. Just a few more months and I can sleep normally.

December 19th

I got a good bird last today—a See-See Partridge. It's larger than the common quail and smaller than a grouse. There are no distinctive markings and its behavior is a creeping traipse across rocky ground.

I've talked with my geologist friend about the garden, and he wants to team up on expenses.

December 21st

I've gotten frost nip on my dick; that's an unusual injury. I've been running in relatively skimpy shorts, and I didn't realize how cold it actually is outside.

Romney is still trying to whip up the idiot base through talks about war with Iran. He said he would have sent troops in to Iran to recover a drone, which they claim to have shot down. God this man is dangerous.

I hit 50 books for the year today; I'll probably read another couple before the end of the year, but this is two years in a row with 50 plus.

December 22nd

I took a day off from class. I needed the break.

I've been saving up supplies for my attempt at making wine in my room. The chow hall had bottles of sparkling grape juice for Thanksgiving, and I saved a few bot-tles, but I suspect there will be more for Christmas. I'm using the empties for storage once I begin my project.

December 23rd

Happy Festivuz

My dick is almost healed; I took a day off running, and I've been looking at weather forecasts more. I'm also going to start running in the heavier canvas shorts to give myself more insulation. This is the most embarrassing injury I've ever had, and unless I have a problem, I'm not going to the medic.

My parents are prepping a package with various seeds for my garden. This is going to be a fun experiment. My dad asked if I'm planning on residing in Afghanistan permanently.

December 24th

I went to the western wall and watched some little kids playing today. There is a place I can look out without worrying about sniper fire. The older ones were harassing the younger ones by throwing rocks at them and pushing them down a steep hill. Bullies are bullies in any culture.

We have Christmas dinner tonight.

When discussing class with one of my Persian friends, I was told I have to be hard on these students, because it's the only thing they are used to. I figured it's worth a shot with Dod Saleem. Tonight, I pointed a spray bottle of cooking oil at him and told him I would shoot him if he didn't spell a word correctly. He spelled it correctly.

December 25th

Christmas Dinner wasn't too bad. It was the same food we had for Thanksgiving. I'm sure I've gained 3 pounds worth of stuffing and egg nog.

I decided to cancel class since it was a holiday, but I invited my students to come hang out and eat with me. Rahman was the only one to come.

I'm preparing to work off yesterday's gluttony. A five-mile run here or a five-mile run at home—no difference beyond the IED this morning. The time difference allowed me to call most everyone I cared about for Christmas Eve.

December 26th

We are going shooting today. The ASG guards and a few contractors have a competition at the old range. It's outside the base, so this is really the first time I've been outside the wire without the benefit of the RG.

Later...

I didn't compete; this is only my second time firing an AK-47, so it would have been pointless against a bunch of prior-army/marines. Twenty people contributed $20, and they received $180 and $120 for first and second place. It was interesting that the buy in was so large. For the contractor's it was less than one hour's worth of pay. For the Afghans, it was more than a day's pay.

I was an awful shot, and I'm not afraid to admit it. With my first 15 round magazine, I made only 5 on the paper target, and only 2 would have been kill shots. My second magazine wasn't much better with 8 out of 15 on the paper and 3 kill shots. Just for fun, on my last magazine, I went for fully automatic; I failed to even hit the paper. All of that was with no pressure of being killed or needing to kill anyone else. Of course the competitors didn't have pressure either, but they all managed to get their rounds on the paper. I do like the AK-47 though. Cleaning it out afterwards, I found it to have an intuitive design that was easy to dismantle and put back together with no real instruction, while the M-16/M-4 is more intricate and temperamental. The common saying is that an AK can be left in a mud puddle for 15 years and afterwards, fired with the most minimal of maintenance, and while the M-16 needs a professional armorer, the AK can be repaired with a tin can and a screw driver. That's probably exaggeration, but these AKs were decades old, and I was impressed with the fluidity of their inner workings, while the M-16s we fired in basic training were just as old and locked up every few rounds. At least with the M-16, I managed to get 43 out of 50 on target.

I don't have an opinion on which rifle is better, but either way, no excuse and/or commentary on West v. East can justify 5 out of 15.

December 30th

Karzai is allegedly cracking down on security contractors in Afghanistan. I'd argue it's only a start.

December 31st

There were 566 coalition deaths in 2011 which is down from the all-time annual high of 711 deaths in 2010. This amounts to a 20 percent decrease in year-to-year deaths after seven successive years of increase since 2003. Of this year's 566 deaths, 495 were from hostile action which means that 12 percent were from accidents or natu-ral causes. This number is significantly down from wartime averages of nearly one in five deaths caused by non-combat incidents. Nine out of twelve months were equal to or less than monthly totals from last year.

Despite the significant drop in total deaths, July is the deadliest month on record for Americans with 71 deaths and the third deadliest year on record for all troops with 82 deaths. Approximately 5,200 US troops were wounded which is only a slight drop from last year's estimates of 5,250. I can find no firm data to analyze wounded troops from other countries, but with the slow withdrawal of many coalition partners, those numbers are largely irrelevant.

8

JANUARY 2012

January 1st

It will really be a sink-or-swim year for the ANA, but most of the ANA seem in good shape. At times they may be a little lazy, but most are competent and enthusias-tic. All ethnic groups have been pushed into working with each other, and I can't help but hope that 10-15 years of working side by side has at least broken down some of the ethnic distrust and maybe also helped built a little bit of rudimentary camaraderie and nationalism. Consider how integration in the US military helped pave the way for a shift in American culture. While we certainly have racism 60 years later, how much worse would it have been without the actions taken by President Truman?

Afghanistan doesn't have the luxury of 60 years. American integration rode the wave of prosperity as we emerged unscathed and wealthy from WWII, while Afghanistan has entered its fourth decade of war. If the Afghans want peace and prosperity, the onus is on them to continue the work we've done over the last 10 years and figure out how to get past their differences. With the rise in literacy and the beginnings of a middle class, Afghanistan possesses its own destiny. As an international community we can continue to guide them, and we can facilitate arrangements with regional powers. In the end it will be Afghans who are just now coming of age that decide whether to fall back into civil war or finish rebuilding their country.

January 2nd

Things have been quiet for a while. New Years passed with no fanfare beyond a couple of flares shot around midnight. It seemed like the year was off to a slow start, but in truth, we've already lost someone just two days in. An SF guy was killed nearby. These are the best of the best, and anytime one is lost, America is weakened. Many can speak two or even three languages, and they are trained to endure privations, which seem glamorous in Hollywood, until one realizes that in real life, the mud is filled with parasites, and there is not a shower waiting just off the set. There is no glamor—just filth and heartache.

The internet is down until the family has been notified. It's a minor inconvenience for us that saves unspeakable pain for the people back home. Without the blackout on communication, those who relish being the bearers of bad news would take to Facebook, e-mail, and Twitter, and as the rumor mill turns, families back home have to wait for final confirmation from the powers that be. It's hard enough to deal with death without having to wait for the official news.

January 3rd

The recent death brought on a discussion with a coworker about funeral detail.

This job demands a level of bearing and discipline beyond the typical expectation we all have. I've only been to one military funeral, but I've heard tales that make one laugh, cry, or angry just from second hand knowledge. The two tales that stand out are simple but either shocking or hilarious. In one funeral, the family played "Prop Me Up Beside the Jukebox (If I Die)" as the coffin was lowered into the grave, and in another, it had rained for days and the pallbearer slipped into the grave. He climbed out with the aid of a fellow airman, stood up, assumed his position and went on, ignor-ing the mud and bruises.

My coworker spent time on funeral detail with the Marines. He said each family reacts so differently. In one funeral, the wife cursed the flag bearer holding the symbol of what she perceived as a wrongful death. In another, the family remained completely stoic until taps played, and they lost all control. As soon as the last echoes of the mournful dirge faded they fell back into their stoicism and only a few tears were left to show what had happened. The most bizarre was the family that invited the entire funeral detail to a barbecue after the funeral and partied the rest of the day.

I like the idea of someone partying after I die—of people getting wasted on my behalf, and I sure as hell hope they don't pour any booze out on my behalf; why waste it?

I should go ahead and pick the photo I want for my after-party just in case. You gotta be prepared.

January 4th

Today was the first winter day that I can classify as miserable. While the 12-degree temperature wasn't awful, the wind blasted us with a mixture of sand and sleet that made all but a quick sprint to the chow hall or bathroom impossible. There is a blizzard just north of us.

January 5th

I am continuing class but there are no great developments at this time. Sergeant Major Khan has returned from some well-deserved rest in his home province, and he's back with a vigor that has over-shadowed Rahman. Unfortunately, Rahman does not have the background in reading and writing that is necessary for the true mastery of a language, and I believe I have taken him as far as I can when it comes to language. He does not see the value in increased literacy, in an occupation that requires mechanical savvy and little else.

January 12th

A video has been released on YouTube showing US military members urinating on corpses; I think it was Marines, but I'm not sure at this time. I don't think much will come of it. There will be a few minor protests in a couple places like Jalalabad, but beyond that, no one will care. Jalalabad is the site of some of the most raucous protests in Afghanistan—a bastion of liberalism, which decries both coalition and Taliban atrocities. The irony is that only the fantastic security provided by the coalition allows them the wiggle room for such evocations of free speech—the same free speech they'll use to denounce our presence. I think the video was from some time a few years ago, so it's also a mitigating factor in the sense that it's already old news.

As for the howling American press, I don't know what we expect to happen when we take a bunch of kids, turn them into professional killers, and then release them to hunt and kill human beings. How does a society rationalize killing another person as noble and patriotic but taking it one step further and abusing the carcass as an abomi-nation? I'm not condoning the desecration, and they should be punished for violating the Laws of Armed Conflict. Our nation does have the burden that comes with being the city on the hill, and that means that we can't get away with allowing people to be-have this way, no matter how poorly the Taliban behave. However, the punishment they will face will equal that of the crime they committed, and it serves no purpose to turn them into monsters when they aren't.

Psychologically, there is no difference between corpse desecration and "excessive celebration" in a football game—15-yard penalty; first down; game on.

January 13th

In an amusing twist of events, the Taliban has said it won't let the urination video derail peace talks. Of course, in a country where constant warfare has devalued human life to the point that people shrug their shoulders when entire families get wiped out, this type of act doesn't really draw negative attention. However, if we were to desecrate the Koran? Just the notion that that idiot in Gainesville, FL might burn a Koran caused trouble for the coalition; I can't imagine what would happen if someone did that here.

January 15th
There has been a rash of missing socks in the laundry facility run by local nationals. I suspect it's carelessness on the part of the Americans, but the idea of a bunch of Turkmen sitting in a smoky room with sock puppets stolen from Americans makes me laugh.
I think everyone is being a bit paranoid.
January 17th
The Taliban are claiming they shot down a "white helicopter" that was moving supplies and personnel. Usually the Taliban claims al-

most everything and usually they are full of shit, but I've always hated chopper and C-130 rides in country. There is always the magic bullet or in the case of the Taliban, the magic RPG.

One of the funniest stories I ever heard in country was from a contracted pilot from Russia in his 50s. Thirty years after the end of the Soviet occupation of Afghanistan, he has been flying the same flight paths over Afghanistan as he had in the Soviet Air Force. [Heavy Russian Accent] "Don't worry; I know these routes my whole life." He wasn't my pilot, but I always wonder what happens if he has a flashback and starts dodging phantom stingers.

January 18th

There was a huge blast a few miles north of us today. A couple of Americans and an untold number of Afghans were killed. As usual, suicide bombers kill mostly Afghans.

I think I have a kidney stone. My urine is bloody, and I feel like puking. There is a throbbing in my back. The medic is gone right now, so I have to suck it up for now. I'll blame it on the long hours, caffeine, and dry air—anything to deflect from the fact that I don't drink enough water. I'll start pounding water and cranberry juice and hope for the best. The medic will be back in a couple days.

January 19th

A good friend of mine died in a military training accident stateside. I don't know what happened. Rest in Peace Lieutenant Tom Fouke.

[Letter to the Editor: January 19th]

I don't like a heavily militarized society, but I understand that violence is sometimes the answer. My grandfathers served in World War II, my dad served in Vietnam, and my brother currently serves. I was part of Operation Enduring Freedom, and I've returned to that fight as a civilian, because I wanted to get closer to a cause I believe in. I'm in Afghanistan now. I haven't visited my home for more than a week at a time in almost 6 years. That being said, I don't look down on anyone who chooses not to serve, because we all have our own path in life; kudos to you if you are a conscientious objector or just have better things to do—it's fine. However, if you are a so-called "hawk," who wants to take the fight to the enemy, then you should enlist. If you are eager to punish and maim our enemies, then man a post. If you say, "kill them all and let God sort them out," then do so while looking your maker in the eye.

In the meantime, at the end of our foreign policy is a bunch of kids, who are asked to do the unspeakable, and the human price has been 1,878 dead, 14,342 maimed, and countless psychological casualties, who aren't even aware of what causes their anger, depression, and dying relationships. I understand, that is the cost of do-ing business and freedom does not come free, but that business must be run by a Presi-dent who, as Commander in Chief of the Armed Forces, has either served in the mili-tary or at least holds a certain empathy for those he sends into harm's way. Regard-less of whether or not a president has served, he must be levelheaded and rational enough to avoid war until it becomes a moral imperative or national emergency. He should not go looking for a fight.

It's easy for Mitt Romney to bang the war drums and whip up the righteous fury of his base, because most of them have never served in the military either. However, they do hold a primeval idea that an eye for an eye accomplishes something beyond leaving everyone blind. More importantly, Romney didn't enlist in 1965, and none of his children have ever or will ever put on a military uniform. They have their reasons, and I accept that, but I cannot accept rhetoric that demonstrates a willingness to en-danger our fathers, mothers, brothers, sisters, sons, and daughters without restraint or second thought, when Mitt Romney and his family do not demonstrate an equal willingness to put their lives on the line.

This diatribe is heavy handed, but if I can make only one person consider what I'm saying about upcoming elections, I will feel that I have done my best to abide by I an oath I took to protect my country from all enemies foreign and domestic. That oath doesn't end simply because I took off the uniform.

Steven Specht (USAF 2006-2010)

[Letter Home January 20th]

Dear Sean,

There is some merit to what you are saying about Islam, but remember that Christianity had a 600-year head start on Islam, and they were still having witch trials 300 years ago. Of course there are violent verses in the Koran, but no more than what is in the Bible. Jesus himself said, "I come not to bring peace, but to bring a sword." Even in the last century we have blood on our hands as a culture. The ethnic cleansing in the former Yugoslavian Republics was a manifestation of nationalism, ethnicism, and Christianity combined into a whirlwind of hate. Need I point out that the victims were Muslims? Heck, half the fighting was between Serbians and Croatians, who are ethnically identical except one group was Catholic and the other Eastern-Orthodox. Yes, the Muslims are fighting over bullshit dogma, but based on our actions, I don't think the West is as evolved as we'd like to think.

As far as being here for 10 years and seeing no change, I am seeing plenty of change in the new generation. Some 8 million people are currently enrolled in school.

A pessimist would say that 1/3 of the population in school is just a testament to the size of the youth bulge in Afghanistan, and an optimist will say that an entire genera-tion is capable of a paradigm shift; both are correct.

Paradigm shift is difficult—nigh impossible. Even within the confines of the most powerful and free nation in the world, it took 30 years to see any real measurable change in the black population after the civil rights movement. Whether from linger-ing prejudice from the white majority or a self-righteous chip on the shoulder of a pissed off ethnic group, aside from what was forced upon business and government through affirmative action, no real change was demonstrated until the last 15 years. No matter how you spin it, change takes time. It's also a lot easier to destroy than to build. A house takes 2-6 months to build, but one bulldozer or some dynamite can de-stroy it in minutes. Afghanistan was never prosperous; however, it was peaceful and stable. After 20 years of war and a brain-drain of all the doctors, lawyers, and teach-ers fleeing to other countries, Afghanistan was left with a median age of ~15. Now, we are rapidly approaching a generation. Each year, the size of the population that has completed high school or university increases, which means that each year we con-tinue on this path, we allow young professionals to enter the market, universities, gov-ernment, and military that are more capable than the previous year. The old guard is dying off and being replaced with motivated and educated people trying to build their own nation. Every time I walk into my classroom, I see eureka moments and epipha-nies that things can be better. I'm just one guy, but I feel I've made a noticeable mark on things with my presence, and it makes me confident that the same is being seen across the country. We can downsize our force here. I don't think they are ready to have the training wheels removed entirely, but a small force of western intel, air force, and special operators kept here for another 10 years will provide enough support for them to take control of their country. In the meantime, we can get rid of most of the star-chasing O-5s and above. You and I have both lost our share of friends out here, but I'd like to think that Ben, Brad, and others died for something honorable and valu-able. If you disagree with me, that's fine, but I think a complete pullout now would dis-honor their memory.

I agree; let's downsize the military and pull out troops, but let's do it in places we've already won. The Soviet Union is no more, and while Putin is a pain in the ass, he's a pain in the ass that has been castrated economically and militarily. Let's take the ~40,000 troops we have in Germany and send them home. We can maintain a Mediterranean presence in Italy and an Atlantic presence in Britain, but anything else in Europe is superfluous. We won in Korea. Sure, maniacs run the North, but South

Korean Republic is friendly, democratic, and possesses one of the strongest economies and strongest militaries in the world. If they can't defend themselves after 50 years, they deserve to fall. The same goes for Japan. China may be a threat, but their entire military infrastructure is paid for by the interest we pay on our Chinese debt—a debt developed predominantly because of increased military spending. So the "need" for a "defensive" force in Japan and Korea becomes a self-fulfilling prophecy as China grows stronger and we grow weaker.

Let's also get out of the dictator business. Cheap gasoline in the 90s was nice, but the cost of doing business with monarchies and dictators is unfathomable. It's more than the financial toll of 9/11; it's the soul of our nation. If we abandon domestic principles internationally under the guise of security, then we should just turn our country over to Muslim fundamentalists, because there isn't anything worth fighting for. Of course, pure idealism is just as bad as pure realism. Realism gives us blow-back, and idealism gives us a populace that is pissed off at our presumption of right-eousness. Instead of an either or approach that pits realist hawks against idealist hippies, we should mesh the two policies and only commit our forces when it fits realism AND idealism. I think Libya was an example of that. Removing Ghadaffi was strategically sound (realism). They asked for our help (idealism).

I'm not trying to change your mind. Your mission in Afghanistan has been completely different than mine, so you have a right to your views, but I just wanted to share my perspective.

Steve

January 21st
I'm starting to feel better. I think the kidney stone passed on its own, because the pain has sig-nificantly dulled.
January 22nd
A common complaint from both civilian workers and military members is that Afghans will steal anything that's not nailed down. The women who come to the

127

clinic will steal anything not nailed down when the staff members have their backs turned. I watched young kids at Mirmandab pilfer a medical supply crate and then when the medic came, insist that the stuff they had wrapped up in their blankets belonged to them.

When we let the locals get away with these kinds of actions, it's like a poor parent letting a child get away with something. I don't mean that in a condescending or derogatory way. I've met 16-year-olds in Afghanistan who already have had to be more "man" than I'll ever be. Part of where we've gone wrong in this campaign is not demanding quid pro quo at every turn. You want us to dig a well? Fine. We'll dig a well, but if there are any IEDs along this strip of road, we will come back and fill that well with concrete. You want a school? Fine. Give us two recruits for the ALP who are going to be on guard duty to keep the Taliban from burning it down at night.

As far as the women getting free healthcare in the clinic, if the Taliban were running a free clinic, those ladies would get their hands chopped off. I'm not suggesting we resort to the tactics of the Taliban, but the boxing of ears might periodically be appropriate. As long as we let these people walk all over us, they aren't going to respect someone who can't draw a line in the sand or delineate between acceptable and unacceptable behavior. They get away with it because we let them.

January 24th

I always wonder if our presence is a double-edged sword. On one hand we are a stabilizing force that helps create educational and economic infrastructure while giving the ANA breathing room to steadily improve. On the other hand, we are a destabilizing force with the Taliban and others wanting to expel the "foreign invaders." I never know if we've struck the appropriate balance.

Today is my birthday. I didn't notice it was my birthday until I looked at my watch. So it goes.

January 25th

The number of explosions, controlled or otherwise, has been rapidly increasing. I feel the dull thud in my quarters nearly once an hour. Operations have been high this winter with a continuing pressure placed on the Taliban during a time when both sides, historically, have taken time off. This is the third winter that the coalition has continued heavy operations throughout the winter, and it ensures the Taliban commanders have no opportunity to rest or recuperate. The fruit of this labor is a tally of killed or detained mid-level Taliban commanders. With freedom of movement taken from the Taliban, the local Afghans and the ANA get some breathing room.

January 26th

Another failed marriage. The same Marine is on the same phone every night desperately trying to be civil while is voice is laced with venom. I recognize the tone of voice; I've been there.

"I know."

"I sent them already; I'm waiting on your end."

"Look, as soon as you finish your forms, you get the house."

"I've got things taken care of on my end." [Phone slams]

Most military marriages are young. High school or college sweet hearts combined with young enlistees who met in training and fell in lust. I was older, but I don't think 15 months of separation in the first three years of marriage helped. I can't blame the near constant separation—if anything, we got along better when we were apart. However, being separated did make it easy to ignore major issues for longer than we should have. More importantly, it allowed both of us to seek consolation where we had no business seeking it.

The fact is that my numbers for overall separation are easy compared to what many Marines and soldiers endure. A military member married to a high school sweet heart is usually doomed. Basic training is right after senior prom then a deployment shortly after that—forget it.

While overall divorce rates in America have slowly declined, military divorce rates have increased by nearly 50 percent since 2001 (1). There are numerous resources, ranging from chaplains to civilian volunteers who are available for free confi-dential consultation, but usually people are too stubborn or arrogant to go. There is an idea that they can figure it out on their own—an ignorance that fails to understand that in a conventional marriage, there is a vast array of family, friends, and commu-nity that helps prop up their marriage. To go it alone in the military is foolish; I was a fool.

January 27th

A high level Talib has hinted that the Taliban will work within the confines of the Afghan Constitution to establish an Islamic Republic. As dangerous as an attempt at theocracy may sound, this is actually a step up from previous statements, which refused to recognize any authority in Kabul, which they perceive to be an American puppet. Sometimes political rhetoric becomes political reality. None of this changes the fact that the Taliban is fragmented, and no one leader can be said to speak for everyone. None of this changes the wildcard in Pakistan, which seeks hegemony in the region, whether it is a Karzai government or a Taliban government. This is also the same group of people who killed former Afghan President Rabbani a few months ago.

One of my Afghan students has been acting squirrely lately. I mentioned it to a couple people in charge just to be safe. He seems borderline belligerent to me, and he's gone through some steps one associates with a suicide bomber with his head and beard recently shaved. He's stopped coming to class, and just in general, he gives me the jitters. Even some of our trusted Afghans have families in jeopardy and will lash out at us to pay off a ransom held by the Taliban. I'm considering canceling class altogether for a few days. I hope I'm wrong.

January 28th

I'm not canceling class. I don't want to let fear dictate my behavior. Whatever will be, will be.

January 30th

There have been only a handful of IEDs in the last couple days with deaths hanging just above last January's totals, but still less than 2010. More and more references have been made regarding the Taliban's willingness to enter talks in Doha. Some balk at the idea of negotiation, but it's the only way.

I've managed six consecutive nights of five or more hours of sleep, so I'm feeling good.

[Letter Home: January 30th]

Dear Lauren

I happened upon a quote today that gave me a better understanding of the feel-ings of doubt I periodically have with my mission here (personal and military).

"We're willing enough to go all the way for them, but we've got this prob-lem—how can you render the duties of justice to men when you're afraid they'll be so unaware of justice they may destroy you."

This is the commentary from the dermatologist who dyed the skin of a white jour-nalist in 1959 so the journalist could experience what it was like to be black in the south—chronicled in *Black Like Me*.

Sometimes I feel I am delusional when I say I can have any positive impact here. Things are so utterly upside-down that what I perceive to be good may only turn out to cause more problems for these people, or even worse, that a promise delayed will be perceived as betrayal. All I know is that I know no other way, and if I get killed in the process, so be it. Some dim platitude won't comfort me in the fleeting moments of con-sciousness and my nobility will be equal in its futility and stupidity as that of a suicide bomber who thinks he's dying to protect his family—oh well.

This rant is manifested itself after a scare over the last few days, in which one of my former students began acting erratic—unfriendly, depressed, and borderline hostile. I say former student, because during all of this, he stopped coming to the English class. I think his presence in class was coerced by his Afghan Sergeant Major who is currently on leave, so I understand his absence, but I did not understand the other behavior. After a few days of it, I became concerned enough that I notified the civilian in charge of external security as well as the Marine in charge of things internally. I also went through paranoid routines of actually using a flashlight at night, ensuring my door was always secured, and carrying a few tennis ball-sized rocks in my pockets—especially while teaching class. The last is the most humorous in that I had convinced myself that if he came in with a gun, I could somehow disarm him or if he came in with an S-vest, I could at least cause a premature det that would leave me maimed but alive.

It was all for nothing. The soldier is back to his normal self. I still don't know the cause of his angst, and I'm glad it was a false alarm, because he strikes me as a truly decent fellow. It doesn't change the fact that I had legitimate safety concerns that go far beyond my usual acts of paranoia.

Am I crazy?

Steve

January 31st

There were 35 coalition deaths in Afghanistan, slightly elevated from last year but still far less than 2010.

1.   Becerra, Leah, 2011, Military Divorce Rate Rises but So Does Support
http://www.veteransunited.com/spouse/military-divorce-rate-rises-but-so-does-support/

9

FEBRUARY

February 1st

I've started a correspondence course for Pashto with a friend. It's a 10-minute audio file along with a written copy. I've gotten through the alphabet, and I've moved on to better lessons.

[Letter Home: February 1st]

Dear Lauren

I've put a lot of thought into [facilitating killing] but when I see how our enemies behave, I can sleep at night knowing the world is a cleaner place. I know there is a gray area, and sometimes innocent people get killed, but in general, we get the right guys. I'm not a fan of bullies, and I don't think much of people who beat up girls trying to go to school or kidnap people so their family members become desperate enough to blow themselves up.

Your comments on pity bring me to a quote from *Black Like Me*.

"Paternalistic—we show our prejudice in our paternalism—we downgrade their dignity."

I think at times we are guilty of this attitude, an extension of the patronizing "white man's burden" attitude of the colonial era. Fast forward to now and it has become the West's burden—no less patronizing and exceedingly ignorant of conditions in the modern world. How do we balance the realism of security with the idealism of brotherhood, while doing so from a position free of condescension? I've seen myself guilty of being overly paternalistic in my English classes, and when I recognize it, I nip it in the bud, but it begs the question of why our default behavior is that of an adult talking down to a child? Whether workers, villagers, or ANA, these are grown people and they should be treated as such. Not knowing how to read and write because you've never been taught is not the same as stupid.

I didn't feel like running today, so I wiled away my free time with literature and some research on the American University of Afghanistan in Kabul. It's a pretty interesting institution, and I wonder if I might continue my mentoring there...

Steven

February 2nd

This was the first time I saw the violent surge of stormy weather that I had expected for monsoon season in Afghanistan. In a matter of minutes, we went from sunshine and clear skies to torrential rain pounding against the metal roof of our containers. Thunder shook the buildings and lightning split the sky. Finally, the roar of rain culminated with ice pounding against the roof. Even now, when stepping outside, there is a mix of rain and dust blown horizontally by gusts up to 40 miles per hour. In the valleys below, the rain is flooding the banks of creeks and rivers, which will provide ample fertilizer for fields but demolish anything in its path.

February 3rd

My run was tough today with yesterday's rain soaking everything and adding about a pound of mud to each shoe. I slipped and splattered mud over my left leg and most of my shorts—funny.

Everything outside that isn't covered in gravel is a mud bath after a slow drizzle over the last 24 hours.

An Afghan in a military uniform shot another coalition member. Nothing to say but the obvious—how it creates distrust and paranoia and increases the opportunity for friendly fire with everyone on edge. Of course, while there are relatively few cases of this sort, the media feeds off these incidents and blows them out of proportion. There have only been a few dozen attacks like this in the entire war. If we consider the hundreds of thousands of police, military, and armed civilians in close proximity to tens of thousands of coalition troops, the number of attacks becomes quite small.

February 4th

I ran into some ANA SF from Mirmandab today. They've moved on to a location farther north, and they were moving out, so I only had two minutes of loud banter and hugging before they took off in their pickup trucks.

[Letter Home: February 5th]

Dear Lauren,

It's ironic that we need reminding of why we don't like something, but I understand where you're coming from. I'm annoyed more than ever at the commercialism in the US when I come back from Afghanistan. I feel my 20-foot container is positively luxurious, and when I go home and hear about people complaining about housing prices, my first thought is, "no one said you had to have wall-to-wall carpet." The average home size was once about 800 square feet. Now it's 1,500. Of course, in addition to the simple math that twice the home means twice the price, it creates an undue demand on materials and labor, which means, in terms of basic economics, prices go up. Shall I even bother to mention the extra cost of upkeep, cooling, heating, and electricity? I pick on the housing market, because that is where the most money goes, but whether it's phones, new car leases, or designer jeans; the wasted money on "stuff" is pathetic. I understand the need for some amount of luxury, but when you have nothing but luxury, the various things have no meaning. Just as evil is necessary to understand good, frugality is necessary to understand luxury.

It's good that your office is preparing for a responsible handoff to the next group. Your replacement needs to understand what has happened over the last year. One of the ramifications of the way we have fought over here is that every 3, 6, 9, or 12 months entire groups rotate out, and we continually reinvent the wheel. While it may be good for the psychological health of a service member to rotate out, it's to the detri-ment of the war. A team builds six months of rapport with locals, and then they leave, replaced by a completely new set of faces. I don't think it's reasonable to expect a local elder to trust the new guy. Of course, the way we did things in Vietnam was the ex-treme opposite, where individuals often replaced individuals; each did their year, and went home. I think there is room to change things up a bit so that we do deployments at a platoon level. That way, there will be a constant rotation of new bodies, but not en-tire teams, so there is a continual new flow of people but enough time to maintain a constancy of operations. Maybe it's not cost effective to do something like that, but it's something to think about. I believe in World War II, you stayed in until you'd built enough points to get out. If you wanted to make the military a career, you had to stay over the war.

I think my team better understands how the handoff needs to occur, and they started the process as soon as they arrived in country. By that, I mean they are already emailing and conferencing relevant background information on continuing op-erations. When the next team gets here, they should be able to continue the mission without any hiccups.

I was incredibly happy yesterday to run into some old students. They were just passing through the area. It was nice to get a hug even if they were wearing body armor. That is something I enjoy about Afghan culture is how close they tend to be. I'll admit that even I am sometimes taken aback at the enthusiasm of an Afghan hug.

I had no opinion on bacha bazi (child prostitution) simply because I think there is a matter of moral relativity that has to be applied. In a country where it is seemingly okay or at least only marginally taboo, the psychological trauma is low. However, the psychological trauma of a teenage woman being seen naked by a non-family member would be devastating. So while the young boy can be physically violated with no lasting ill effects, but what we would consider a minor embarrassment in the US would be devastating.

You made a clever comparison to the "oversexualization" of young girls in America. We can parade 6-year-olds around in thongs and rouge, but a pat on the bottom is crossing the line? Yes. Why? Because our culture has made the arbitrary decision that it's wrong. I saw a humorous but valid editorial that essentially stated. "Ameri-cans think Muslims disrespect their women by forcing them to cover up; Muslims think Americans disrespect their women for forcing them to parade about immod-estly." Of course it is more complicated than that, but it's something to think about.

I have a "small" selection of porn that I got from someone else's hard drive. It is a useful tool, but I agree with your judgment that it can provoke a false sense of reality. I put it in these terms. I don't watch the Super Bowl and suddenly think that I can throw a 50 yard touchdown pass, but after watching porn, we (especially men) have it in our heads that we can do some absurdly difficult sexual act or that every single woman is just waiting to have her skimpy clothes ripped off by the first man who comes along.

Tonight was a wonderful evening. I did a 22-minute run in the moonlight before work. It's interesting the odd looks the Turkmen gate guards give me as I head out. Even the daylight runs spark blatant look of bemusement, but they really look at me strangely when I run at night. Of course Turkmen in general fit none of the stereo-types of Afghanistan. I have trouble pinning them down.

It's interesting that Afghans seem to be such a warrior culture, but only when it comes to hand to hand combat and some hand-eye coordination. Hell, a Hazara took bronze in the 2008 Olympics in one of the martial arts. However, some of the other athletic events seem bizarre to them. I've never seen an Afghan run unless it was an emergency. Of course the fact that girth is still a sign of wealth and prosperity might have something to do with the lack of physical prowess and inversely, the fact that so much of the country has little time for leisure has something to do with it as well. The austerity does create some interesting games, including a national past time among im-poverished youth, which consists of using a small rock to knock another small rock off a boulder or wall. My humorous tale of participation was back in Mirmandab. After several half-hearted attempts to knock the small rock off a low patch of masonry, I grew bored and hurled a baseball-sized chunk of granite. I completely missed the small rock, but by shattering the entire wall, thus knocking the small rock from the wall. About half the Afghans were congratulating me and patting me on the back for creativity and the other half glared at me for cheating. I can't please them all I suppose.

Regarding cultural sensitivity, since you are a woman, some of the cultural rules go out the window, and since you are a modern American white girl most likely talking to enlightened, westernized Afghans, there aren't many strict rules to follow. In my entire time here, I've only had two Afghans give me the impression of being pushy regarding culture, religion, politics, etc. Every other encounter has been from the position of mutual respect and understanding and on the sticky issues, an ability of agreeing to disagree.

I know local women tend to be very deferential to their husbands, but there is a significant minority of men who are completely henpecked and allow the livestock [see note] to rule over them (their word not mine) I'm in Helmand, which is the most backward place in the entire country. If you are in a major city like Kabul, it's probably more progressive than a rural town in the Deep South (of America).

Sorry to keep it so ambiguous, but I'm seriously not sure of how to answer your question on culture.

Steve

*A common term for women and small children in Pashto is "animals." February 10th

I had fun harassing Rahman tonight. As a linguist, I am amused about the constant debates between various Pashtuns about what constitutes "pure Pashto." Of course there are no languages completely free of outside interference, but for a country like Afghanistan, which has been crossroads of every culture in Eurasia, to claim any sort of linguistic purity is asinine. Najib was arguing on behalf of Kandahari Pashto. He insisted that Kandahari was pure and all the others had been muddled by time. Without hesitation, I drew a tree on the white board and asked Najib what it was called in Pashto, and he called it "drakhta," while my Eastern students all called it "wana." "Wana" is the arguably "pure Pashto" word used only in Pashto while "drakhta" is a Farsi loan word that has permeated not only Pashto, but also Uzbek, Turkmen, Urdu, and Hindi among others. Now I harass him and call him a "Farsiwan" which means he is a Farsi speaker. It would be an insult if I was a stranger but I can get away with it.

February 11th

I did a decent 60-minute run today, and I've found a partner interested in completing a marathon here at FOB Robinson.

February 12th

Thinking back to the issue of wild dogs in Afghanistan and the rampant amount of rabies, it's interesting to find out that SPC Kevin Shumaker died from rabies in

August after being bitten by a dog in Afghanistan. It's only been recently reported stateside, but I've heard rumors about it for a few weeks. What an awful and meaningless death.

February 15th

Today was the first obvious sign of warming weather. It's cold, but not as cold as usual, and I think I feel a warm breeze.

We are halfway through February, and there are only five coalition deaths. We are looking at the lowest total casualties since February 2007 if we maintain this casu-alty rate.

In other news, there have been 3,021 civilian deaths this year with only 187 at the hands of coalition forces. That's six percent. I hope that the rising civilian casualties at the hand of insurgents works in our favor, but these things can be tricky.

February 17th

[Presidents] Ahmadinijad, Karzai, and Zardari met in Pakistan to discuss regional security, but nothing came of it. I don't think anyone ever thinks that anything will change. It was mostly Ahmadinijad posturing and mouthing off about "imperialism" in the region without directly mentioning the United States.

[Letter February 18th]

Dear Lauren,

This is the second round of weather that I think can definitely be contributed to the monsoon. It rained for almost 36 hours and the amount of clouds in the sky indicate that it could start again. I suppose it's no different than the summer rain storms back home in North Florida, except of course Florida gets rain year round with a short dry spell in the fall. Rain is still an unusual phenomenon to me in Helmand. I'm considering going swimming in the pit we use to fill our HESCO Barriers, just to say I swam in Afghanistan. I think it would be quite funny even if I was the only one laughing.

I have class in a few moments; well, dinner and then class. I've found that my literacy student gets overwhelmed so quickly, that we only do about five minutes of work at a time. He is at a point now where learning is up to him. He needs to practice in his quarters and with the Afghans who can read. I'll continue with him until I leave, because I said I would, but there is only so much a nonnative can help him with. It's funny how much technology helps with learning. If he were in the US, even at the lowest socioeconomic level, he'd have an iPod or at least a CD player, so I could burn an audio file with the top 1,000 most common words and he could play it over and over again.

Is it silly to feel somewhat guilty that the bottom rung of society in America has better access to education than most of the world? The blame rests primarily on the Muslim clerics, who espouse a view that reading isn't important, but to some extent, the US government perpetuated and fostered those maniacs in the Cold War. I have to believe the problem is far worse than it would have been otherwise. The results of events that took place before I was born have manifested themselves now that I'm an adult, and while I'm not responsible, I feel it is a sins-of the-father type situation.

Are you frustrated at the rhetoric from [politicians] that they are tired of [Obama and Clinton] apologizing for America? Maybe it's just my hippie-liberal brainwashing, but I was taught that when you make a mistake, you admit it. It's part of being an adult. I wonder how much of our international problems would go away with an apology.

"Dear Iranian government, we did things during the Cold War that we perceived to be necessary for our national survival, and a lot of people got hurt. We aren't making an excuse for our actions; we are just giving the reason for them. Then, when you lashed out at us for our actions, rather than admit the mistake initially, we perpetuated the same policy, because the blowback occurred in the climax of the Cold War. Hindsight is 20-20, but at the time, no one really knew that the Soviet Union was going to fail. If we could go back and do things differently we would, but we can't. That got us off on the wrong foot. We've continually revisited our differences with rhetoric, propaganda, and a show of force. We even articulated that you would be the next country invaded after invading Iraq, and then we invaded Iraq. We've screwed up. We don't know how we got here, but it's not a good place. Maybe we should both sit back and chill out for a second and re-evaluate things. Is there really anything to be fighting over?"

I don't see how apologizing affects our national security. The worse case scenario is that Iran gets squirrely and we wipe out their entire defense infrastructure with a squadron of F-16s and the 5th fleet. The best-case scenario is that both countries can move on to more important things.

Steve

February 19th

Well, I've officially gone swimming in Afghanistan. The quarry used to fill HESCO barriers had about four feet of water in it—more than enough to do a good breaststroke. It was, however, covered with a half inch of petroleum runoff from the fueling station, and the smell is not coming out of my clothes or hair. I also have a massive headache.

There is a truly bizarre story coming out of Kandahar about a guy who pretended to be a Senator and gained access to a lot of systems and offices where he shouldn't have been. The Taliban is not claiming responsibility, so it is likely Iran or Pakistan. If he's a foreigner, I hope the Taliban get to him before we do. Most of them have grown weary of foreign meddling, and they'd probably get more out of him than we could. Whatever they learn, we'll find out eventually anyway.

February 20th

I tripped over my own feet and broke my fall with my face hitting a metal pole. By the time I'd made it back to my room, the blood was streaming down my face from

a cut along the top of my right eyebrow. I trimmed the hair away from the wound and washed it before going back to the office, but it was still bleeding. I walked in with blood trickling along my eye and asked, "Do you think I should get stitches?" It was a pretty funny reaction from the guys in the office; I'll be getting teased about this for some time, so I might as well embrace it and meet it head on by starting off with a joke. The skin was too tight for stitches, so the medic patched the gash with some medical super glue. There will be a small scar beneath the hairline that will be covered up once the shaved area grows back.

February 21st

Some foolish people accidentally burned copies of the Koran in Bagram. Local workers found them halfway through the destruction process and fished them out of the trash. This is not going to be good.

[Letter Home: February 22nd]

Dear Sheryl,

I feel like I haven't sent you something proper in quite some time, so I hope to remedy that now.

I have just over two months to go now, and I'm eager to get home. I don't think you've ever stayed overseas before, but it's normal to be completely at ease with the passing time until one can see the light at the end of the tunnel, and then the end can't come soon enough. Usually there is some event that triggers the desire to leave. For me it was last week, when I thought I might have a day off, but after being mentally prepped for the first day off in months of 12-hour days, the cancellation of that time off was emotionally crushing. Ever since then, my heart just isn't in it like it should be. I need to find some motivation; these guys deserve my best at all times.

I'm looking forward to being home for more than a week for the first time in six years. It's hard to believe that four years of military and two years of civilian time have gone by this fast. The year in Afghanistan certainly ate up some time. It's also hard to believe that I'm less than a year away from 30. Since 25, I have had to do the math to figure out how old I am, so there is a general indifference to big 3-O, but I guess it's a milestone. Honestly, I didn't expect to make it to 30, so fingers crossed I'll exceed my own dim expectations. At least I outlived Amy Winehouse.

I've cracked the cover on running essays you sent me, and I'm quite excited to see the content I'm looking forward to another attempt at a 50-mile run this summer, and I'll be ready for it. I'm planning on two marathons on the way out of Afghanistan. I'll do one at KAF, and the second one or two days later at BAF. I'll rest up, do some cross training with some long distance swims and be ready to go on a 50 in late June or early July. Of course the terrain will be slightly different in NW Florida, so it won't be quite as difficult as my failed attempt in 2008. I've only been averaging about 18 miles a week right now, but I've been doing at least one long run a week.

Steve

February 24th

I've started the process of wine making. If I'm caught, I'll be fired, but it's a funny experiment. It's probably not worth the risk, but I feel I'm running in circles and want something to pass the time. There has been absolutely no juice in the chow hall, so I've decided to go with some chopped fruit, Capri Sun, and white sugar. I suspect it will be completely undrinkable, but I'm more concerned with the chemistry of it than I am the final product. I did make a batch a few years ago with Kool-Aid, and that was marginally drinkable as long as I held my breath. This batch is chopped strawberries, chopped pineapple, a couple cups of white sugar dissolved in water I boiled with a teapot and four servings of Capri Sun. I have yeast I brought from home.

For now I'm letting it bubble in a Tupperware container. The plastic should give it an excellent bouquet.

February 25th

The Koran burning last week is a convoluted issue. It would appear that the Korans had been used to smuggle information and contraband in the detention facility in Bagram. Prisoners would write in the margins of the Korans as if they were taking notes on verses and then share those Korans with others. It is, in fact, Taliban prisoners who have desecrated the Koran, but the coalition has made the blunder in disposing of them as they would garbage. While it would be acceptable to burn the defaced Korans, someone should have had the common sense to round up a few sympathetic clerics and have them take care of the issue. It was an honest mistake I'm sure, and as of yet, no coalition forces have paid the price. There have been several Afghans wounded or killed in protests outside of BAF and a few Taliban blasts that targeted the throngs of people.

February 26th

I'm working on making some audio files of the most common English words. It's primarily for Rahman so he can practice his reading by looking at the paper copy of the words while listening to me say them slowly and clearly. I'll burn the files to a CD and pass it around to the surprising number of Afghans with laptops.

Rahman's brother is working on the camp now. It makes sense from a security standpoint. Rahman has proven himself to the Americans, so his brother is probably not a security threat if Rahman vouches for him. Of course a reduced security threat doesn't necessarily mean competence. My friend Fingers at Mirmandab vouched for his nephew and his brother in law, and neither of them were very productive.

February 27th

It's been a week since the Koran burning. The media continue to grasp at straws, attributing normal levels of violence to the Koran burning. There have been some protests, but the rate of attacks has remained the same.

February 29th

The Arabs have been testing their artillery for days. I get 2-3 hours of uninterrupted sleep at best and then the pounding wakes me up—oh well.

At 27, this month will be the lowest number of coalition deaths since May of 2009.

10

MARCH

March 1st

    I'm bottling my first and probably only attempt at making hooch in my room, but I can't cap it for a while. It will make approximately six glasses when all is said and done, but based on the smell; I suspect it isn't going to taste very good. Professionals would bottle it with an airlock to let the remaining gas escape. Amateurs would use a party balloon wrapped around the neck and accomplish the same effect. I have a plastic bag. I should have planned better—oh well.

March 3rd

Jupiter, Venus, and the moon have converged into one unit for the time being, and when combined with the sunset looking over the Helmand River and the Sangin Valley; it is an exquisite view.

[Letter Home: March 6th]

Dear Lauren,

Well, I'll tell you a more in depth account of what I've been up to lately.

I've started my garden, though I wish I had started it two weeks ago, as the weather has been quite warm as of late. So far, I've planted radishes, tomatoes, a mix of two lettuces and endive. I still need to plant goosefoot, and I have some broccoli and cauliflower seeds, but I don't think I'm going to mess with them, because they require higher maintenance. I will probably plant another round of tomatoes and lettuce, but I haven't made that decision yet.

My library is coming along nicely, and it's expanded beyond the boundaries of the initial bookshelf I stole. A bunch of donations have come in, the total number of books is well beyond 300, not counting the stash in my room that I'll donate before I leave. I think I'll have to build some shelves. I'd like to be able to section it off into fiction, nonfiction, religion, and magazines/games/audio books.

Steve

March 8th

They are opening an all girls' internet café in Kabul.

There is so often a push for women to have equal access to everything men have, but in reality anything beyond "separate but equal" will not work in this country, at least not in the short term.

Few would argue that slavery in America was a good thing, but I think anyone understands that the nation would not have survived if the founding fathers had attempted to abolish the practice. An attempt to abolish the practice would have failed, and it would have taken the nation with it.

In Afghanistan, there is such a strong push to have women's rights, but when it is a society living on crumbs, "equal rights" merely means an equal share of the crumbs. If we can build a framework for a society that will eventually liberalize at its own pace, it will be far more successful. If we try to transplant a western worldview in all things, we are doomed. Let us transplant a western military and economy, and liberalization will come with the rise of the middle class.

Build the infrastructure that allows women to ameliorate themselves. Access to segregated schooling and segregated internet means better education and more information. That allows them to make better decisions, and their daughters will change the country.

March 7th

I met a remarkably kind and inquisitive Arab which softened my generally intolerant view of Gulf Arabs. His prejudice was amusing, in that he assumed all Americans are Christian, but as we discussed Islam, he changed his assumption and accepted that I must be Muslim. When he found out I was neither Muslim nor Christian, he was too flabbergasted to query further and we fell into a linguistic discussion of Arabic.

We are all guilty of prejudices, but only through confrontation and exposure to those that break our stereotypes can we learn how wrong we are.

March 9th

It appears that Parwan prison [note] will be slowly turned over to the Afghans in the next few months. This is an important stepping-stone in empowering the Afghan government and letting them take over their own country.

March 10th

One of the most important things we can do is to encourage regional capitalism. This is, of course, already happening with nations vying for an opportunity to exploit Afghanistan's mineral wealth. Exploitation means infrastructure and development. Infrastructure and development mean jobs and wealth. Wealth means education.

[Letter Home: March 10th]

Dear Andrea,

I can't sleep, so you'll pardon me for contacting you with random thoughts and

It's funny to contemplate insomnia and consider that only the luxuries of the modern world allow us to hit the pillow with enough energy to suffer insomnia. I went for a short 21-minute run which rounds out 230 minutes for the week and more than enough to make my goal of 1,000 miles this year. I did a 90-minute run on Thursday and said I'd take a week off, but my legs were twitching, and I had to burn off some en-ergy.

I've been increasingly frustrated at the irresponsible media coverage of this war. They want it to sell newspapers and invigorate interest, but they are trying to make it into Vietnam—it isn't. There is a concerted effort to cast Obama and Bush as some hideous conjoined-twin love child wrought by a monstrous union between Nixon and LBJ—they aren't. Aside from a bumbling Texas governor and an "honorable end to the war," there are no similarities; go away, there is nothing to see here. They want a [My Lai] massacre to keep people in front of the screens, but when Guantanamo and

Abu Ghraib couldn't get the job done, they resorted to exaggeration and simply mak-ing up stories of rape and desecration, so when rape and desecration occurs, it is par for the course instead of an anomaly.

All I want for Christmas is Olberman's head on a pike; bring me the former edi-tor of Newsweek too.

Steve

PS: Andrea, It's with abashed irony that I wrote my previous letter one day be-fore a US soldier in Kandahar walked off base and massacred an entire family. I loathe condemning too soon. Perhaps there is an explanation, but I have my doubts.

There is nothing to be done but pick up the pieces of shattered morale and rap-port and rebuild them.

Steve

March 11th

It's strange that the fallout from the soldier deliberately massacring a dozen peo-ple is less than the furor over a few burned Korans. What a weird place.

I've decided to order eight copies of *The Black Stallion* for my class. Horses are historically important in the lore of Afghanistan, so for those able to read it, it should hold their interest. Only a few of them are at that level of reading, but I think it will be a good gift to leave with them along with some good dictionaries. My main excuse for buying this is because I want to leave Rozi with lots of literature, but I'm leery of buy-ing him something and leaving others out.

Installations across the country had a shakedown of dorm rooms. Evidently the soldier in Kandahar had stockpiled a bunch of ammunition in his room, so we had to endure a "health and wellness" inspection. I hadn't disposed of my wine, and I don't think my heart has ever beaten so fast. They appeared to ignore it, and this evening I dumped it out. I was unable to see, sniff, sip, or summarize—a great tragedy.

March 12th

One of the most amusing and surreal things I've seen in Afghanistan occurred to-day. Some of the Afghan workers were playing a video game that featured Navy Seals killing Taliban. I wonder if this should be a training tool to condition people to killing the Taliban. Some in the US blame video games for violence in America, so it's worth a shot.

I'm hoping Rozi can keep the class going when I leave; I'll have to talk Bob about it, but I feel better about leaving my class behind for someone else to take over.

March 13th

I replanted tomatoes and lettuces. I don't know why they didn't grow. I'm going to prop the canisters up in a different manner that increases sunlight. The radishes are doing well.

I've begun to count the days. I'll be out of here in approximately two months.

March 14th

Karzai is lashing out and throwing a tantrum, but I have to wonder, how much of this is scripted. It would make sense that it is scripted given. Many of his demands are for things that are already in play. We are already planning a troop draw down, so demanding a reduction in troops allows him to look like the guy in charge. I'm sure that some of his outbursts are not planned; those are the laughable ones. There was a 2009 speech where he ranted about the foreigners destroying the precious air quality of Kabul with too many helicopters and jets. I'm sure it isn't good for the environment, but it is probably the 2 million 1992 Toyota Corollas doing most of the poisoning.

March 15th

The Taliban have pulled out of the pending Doha peace talks in the wake of a series of screw-ups by the coalition forces. They are viewing all of this as a propaganda coup, but I think they are making a huge strategic blunder. Admittedly, in the interim, our reputation will be damaged by news of corpse desecration, the Koran burning, and this most recent massacre, but in the long term, we are going to continue to kill midlevel Taliban commanders while continuing to develop the ANA, ALP, and other forces that can carry on after we are gone. The Taliban will re-enter peace talks at a later date, but they will do so from a weaker position in negotiating for their place in the political process. Someday, in the next five years, they will be nothing more than a political party, perhaps with an armed wing like Hamas or Fatah, but if they pushed right now, they would argue from a position of strength; as it stands, they can only get weaker. I'm excited about the possibilities.

March 16th

I am frustrated about western media continuing to rally around the massacre. In the meantime, Taliban IEDs have killed nearly four-dozen Afghan civilians, and 12 Turks have given their lives for this war effort. I'm revolted about the events of last week as much as anyone else, but they don't erase the work we have done or the work we are continuing to do. Most importantly, putting the news about 12 Turkish soldiers getting killed on the back page is yet another insult to our coalition partners.

The families of the victims in Kandahar will be compensated in a place where death is an everyday occurrence. Few in Afghanistan will remember the incident in a year from now.

The media have made several theories including traumatic brain injury, financial problems, and revenge.

March 17th

A guy from my hometown died today. As he graduated high school long after me, I didn't know him. Army SPC Daquane D. Rivers died in Paktia province from a non-combat related incident. He wanted to join the military to get ahead in life, according to my hometown newspaper.

March 20th

It's the Persian New Year, which is celebrated by all the non-Pashtuns and many of the Pashtuns. I had a good time hanging out with the Turkmen guards in their compound. The main course was Turkmen flatbread and lamb. The bread was dipped in the meat juice. They also had tea, various sweets, and other things but the meat was exquisite. They gave Bob and me the place of honor at the head of everything, which was quite embarrassing.

As the meal came to a conclusion, they brought out a tambur, a two stringed instrument similar to a banjo. It's amazing how much variety can be sucked out of only two strings. Much of it was similar to power chords from American rock music but at a higher octave with the strings wound tight around the neck of the tambur. At random, Turkmen would start singing in their own language, and I could rarely understand it, but I caught random Dari words here and there about blessings and prosperity for the future year. The most surprising lines were those referencing a beautiful new woman for the New Year with some suggestive hip grinding in rhythm to the music. I was not the only one lost in the language, and when a Hazara had his chance on the tambur, he belted out a few lines in Dari on the fact that he had no idea what they were saying in Turkmen, but happy New Year anyway.

The music picked up in rhythm and a dolay (similar to a bongo) was added to the mix to allow some dancing, which continued in a sexually suggestive manner. Some of the more effeminate men danced as I would expect a woman to dance, but there was no petting or other sexual activity. I think it was merely role-play in the absence of women.

All in all, I appreciate the Turkmen music much more than the Pashtun music. March 21st

English class is developing into something more than I ever imagined it would. According to Bob, the ASG is passing down a requirement that Afghan supervisors must be functional in English, so Rozi will begin teaching in the next few weeks and Bob is asking me to help him create the class. We'll see how this goes.

[Letter Home: March 25th]

Parents,

My garden is a miserable failure, which I secretly expected, though I started with high hopes. Not a thing has grown besides radish plants. I'm sure I've under watered, over watered, or made some other vital mistake that the average 12-year-old Afghan would laugh at as a rookie mistake, but it was fun and a good way to pass the time. My neighbors also tried and had no luck either, so we are missing something.

I still think my idea of taking back the desert has merit. I spoke of spreading annuals and grass seed as a way to help hold the soil, but looking at how green things have gotten post monsoon, I wonder if that would be redundant. So instead, I propose we set up wind breaks made up of eucalyptus (or some native equivalent) as a way of slowing the drive of the seasonal gales that turn this place into a dust bowl on a weekly basis.

Of course it goes without saying that this region has little to no large-scale water management. A series of earthen dams would be interesting though. I don't think the notion of eminent domain would go over well with independent and stubborn Pashtuns.

The ALP seems to be a budding success born from twin failures of the ANP and tribal militias. The tribal militias failed from the complete lack of organization, and we often backed weaker tribes who gave lip service to fighting the Taliban even though they had no local credibility. You might have thought we had learned that lesson in Vietnam, no luck I suppose. The top-down approach of the ANP was a failure for obvious reasons, set up in a nation with little history of central governance, but also, because the ANP failed to move people away from their localities and break up rings of corruption. I've never met an ANA soldier who was from Helmand. I'm sure any ANA recruits from Helmand are sent somewhere else. The ANP fails to move people around. The ALP has limited control of the area surrounding its own villages and it has a sense of ownership for those who want gainful employment and stability in the region, but it doesn't do so much to cater to local rivalries.

It's both amusing and heartbreaking to see the continued fractures along ethnic and tribal lines, but there is little that can be done on that issue. Occasionally, I can delve into that absurdity with the locals when it comes up in class, but I make sure Afghans bring up any critiques of Afghanistan. My students are Afghan Special Forces, and as such, they tend to be more educated and therefore more inclined to question the status quo. By letting them bring up the questions, I slide into a mentoring role, and because they trust me, they are comfortable with my opinions.

I think the powers that be could learn a lot from my approach of holistic engagement at the ground level, and I think I've already left a mark on things. At my previous location, I've been told that the newest MARSOC team has continued teaching English.

Steve

March 31st

Unless we get 12 deaths in the next 3 hours, this will be the fourth month in a row with the lowest number of combat fatalities in three years. I'm always confused at the notion from our free media that there has been a huge uptick in violence from as a result of a Koran burning, other atrocities, or a spring offensive.

APRIL-MAY

April 1st

I visited with the Uzbeks tonight and watched Rozi teach English for a third time. Unfortunately, I smashed my hand in the door of the Humvee, and while the fingers aren't broken, my index and middle fingers will be all but useless for the next two days. I felt awkward, because I didn't want to shake anyone's hand but I didn't want to offend. I spent most of the time showing the wound and explaining I didn't want to get blood on them. It made things really bad when the Mullah insisted on shaking my hand anyway. He squeezed right on the wound and I did my best to not yelp like a child—oh well.

April 3rd

There was a dust halo around the moon tonight, and the Arabs were firing illume rounds. It was almost like a lightshow. Man I love this place.

[Letter on April 3rd]

April 3rd

Dear Lauren,

I can't sleep for shit today, but after taking Tylenol PM two days in a row, so I don't want to take it for a third day. Just a little over a month before I am out of here and on can go back to some semblance of a circadian rhythm.

I was able to cut away most of the dead skin on my injured finger. I always worry about a blood infection with this kind of injury, because it's so easy for nasties to get underneath the flap of skin. Basically the crush of the Humvee door lifted the first several layers of skin away from the flesh, but it didn't disconnect completely like a scrape would; in fact, it was only even open on one small part. There is a name for that, but I can't remember what it's called.

The human body is so amazing. The area closest to the opening has already begun to heal, and can be touched gently without discomfort as the new skin begins to spread. The deepest part (under the recently removed skin) oozes periodically and I have to be careful that I don't get plasma on anything. By this time tomorrow that too will be mostly healed over, and with a vigorous battery of cocoa butter in a month there will be no sign of injury.

Steve

April 5th

My fingers are gradually getting better. Typing is difficult at work but I'll manage.

April 7th

I've discovered a great way to muffle the sound and block the light. I got an old mattress and wedged it against the door. Some of the larger explosions still rattle me awake, but with no light flooding in, I'm able to fall back asleep. I wish I'd discovered this trick earlier.

April 9th

I picked up a bad intestinal bug; I'm blaming the collard greens, but it could have been anything. The gory details aside, I realized halfway through a five mile run that I was done for; I didn't' even try to save the socks and underwear.

[Letter Home: April 10th]

Mom,

I understand how you feel about money. I could come out here for 5 years and be a millionaire, but the ramifications of that would be a very lonely life. I want to have a wife and kids and I want to be able to relax and go a day without hearing gun-fire or an explosion.

On the other hand, I feel an overwhelming sense of duty that I can't shake. I feel like I'm abandoning this place. I don't know ...

One of my student's older brothers had half a magazine of AK-47 rounds emptied into his belly because he was helping Americans. That incident was four years ago, but he's still here. He's dutifully helping us with an open and inoperable wound against his spine. He doesn't get to leave this situation, but it seems unfair that we just keep rotating back to America every 3, 6, 8, 9, or 12 months.

The older brother is a new arrival here. He's a very friendly guy and genuinely likable, but he didn't seem interested in the English lessons; that is sometimes the case with older men. Rahman is my student, and his siblings are typical of post 9/11 Afghanistan. His oldest brother has no education. Rahman has some education, but most of his knowledge is self-taught. His next sibling is studying to be an interpreter. His twin 15-year-old siblings will likely be able to go to college. It's something I've seen repeated several times since I've started teaching. The younger the student, the more opportunities they've had to improve since the coalition started building schools.

I have some exciting news. Well, it's exciting for me, so as you read this, at least pretend to be enthusiastic. Maybe you can give each other a high-five and open a half-finished bottle of wine with a vigor that would allow one to imagine it is a bottle of champagne threatening to spill.

My best student has been asked by his American supervisor (security contractor) to start an English class for the security guards. Rozi has pursued this new task with enthusiasm and the results are stunning. He runs two classes, because there are two guard shifts, and I've had a chance to visit the second shift class. I was amazed at how well they could rattle off the alphabet. I was also amused to see the authoritative side of the normally obsequious Rozi, when one of the students missed the letter and was yelled at in Turkmen to start again, "and this time do it right."

ASG is the name of the contracting company, run by a mixture of foreign contractors and Afghans. They have a requirement that supervisors must speak English, but so far, no one has been able to meet a requirement as realistic as an Afghan Space Program. This local detachment is making waves, and it appears that these English classes are going to be the model for the entire company which will begin classes at other bases. This means hundreds of Afghans, spread across the entire country will be developing linguistic and literacy skills.

Now my job is to train the trainer. I go to Rozi's classes and take notes on his efforts. To some extent I feel like a fraud by doing this, because I don't have an education degree, but after 10 months of teaching, I guess I'm as qualified as anyone. At any rate, I have 10 more months experience than he. At least he can learn from my mistakes.

Rozi continues to diligently attend my class, which is placed shortly before his second shift class, so he's already geared up to use English when he drives down to the ASG compound.

I still feel awkward at the level of respect afforded to me by Afghans. I'd like to think they are appreciative of my efforts, but I think it's more a perception that I'm an authority figure and Muslims tend to have an unhealthy submission to authority bred into them. Everywhere I go I'm greeted with "teacher" or "Ustaz" which is Pashto/ Dari for mentor. Only a few people have the confidence to address me as Steve or "Sher Khan" which is a name bestowed upon me by faculty at DLI. In an actual class, they all stand up when I enter the room. It's their culture, and I'm not here to change it, but I am amused at the stark contrast with American schools where no one would ever stand up for a teacher.

Steve

April 16th

The media is reporting an uptick in violence as a result of the Taliban's "spring offensive."

As it stands, we are looking at yet another month with lower casualties than last year.

I did a half-marathon today and I'm losing another toenail. As of right now, I'm shooting for a full marathon on April 27th which will be a good preparation for three back-to-back marathons I am planning on the way out of here in Kandahar, Bagram, and Kuwait.

[Letter Home: April 20th]

Dear Jasmine,

I'm sorry our phone call was cut off, but I wanted to discuss the "threat" of Iran in more depth. We already have the resources in place with which to dominate Iran if they decided to get squirrely. As we've discussed before, the 5th fleet is located in Bahrain. The fleet isn't a battle ready force unto itself, but it controls American ships in the area, and there is usually one or two carrier groups within a day's trip. A carrier group is a collection of ships that accompany an aircraft carrier. It's usually a handful of destroyers and other ships with a loose assortment of submarines in the area. The submarines aren't specifically tied to the group, but they are around. The navy isn't my specialty, but I do have a general idea about its capability. It's not about the numbers. While Iran might have some carriers, which could cause trouble regionally, their entire carrier force is composed of derelict diesel craft that are so noisy that they'd be eliminated within a few minutes.

Their air force is equally abysmal. Most of their aircraft are from the 1970s and 1980s, but they do have a few aircraft from the 90s. A lot of their main attack force is made up of Russian Mig-29s which are so poorly built that Russia can barely give them away. Many of their planes are American hand-me-downs from a time when we got along. My dad was flying in F-4s in the 1970s. The US got rid of F-4s in all capacities except a few Air National Guard units shortly after the Vietnam War. Iran still uses them. I don't recall the exact year that the US stopped using the F-14, but I believe it was early in Clinton's first term. To put it bluntly, one of Iran's BEST aircraft is a plane that we got tired of 20 years ago.

In addition to American aircraft, all of our "allies" across the gulf would likely get a piece of the action. They might want to sit out the war for diplomatic reasons, but if any of them entered, it would be on our side. Saudi Arabia has one of the largest stockpiles of F-15s in the world; Qatar is armed to the teeth with patriot missiles. UAE, Kuwait, and Bahrain are also armed and trained by Americans.

Finally, it's not about size; it's ultimately about training. Even if we fought "fair" and only matched them ship per ship, man per man, and plane per plane, Iran is so poor that they can't afford to provide quality training to their pilots, soldiers, and seaman. I can give you the best firearm in the world, but if you don't know how to use it properly, it's less useful than a good, solidly built, club.

I'm speaking specifically on the notion of Iran actually misbehaving. The dynamic changes when a country is fighting a defensive war, and while most Iranians are likely not satisfied with their government, it's easy to whip up nationalism when a na-tion is under attack, so actually taking their country might be more difficult than de-fending the area from an Iranian offensive. Realistically though, their SAM batteries would be taken out from afar, and after that, their air force and navy, which we've al-ready discussed. With no air power or sea power, a ground war against conventional troops would be over in a few days. It would be similar to the 100 hours in the first round of the Iraq war.

To what end? Just like Iraq II, we'd be stuck with the cleanup bill. Maybe the Islamic countries could help with the tab, but at a minimum, we'd need a peacekeeping force for a minimum of two years as Iran transitioned from a de-facto religious dictatorship to a secular state. Diplomacy would be far cheaper in the end; we have so much in common with Iran. We both have to deal with East-African oil pirates. We both have to deal with Sunni terrorists. We both have to deal with Taliban and Afghanistan. The only thing standing between us and sitting down with the Iranians, is us. We are too wrapped up in history to effectively deal with Iran on an objective basis, and the [American/Israel Public Affairs Committee] is powerful enough to scare a lot of Congressmen into submission.

George Washington warned us about allowing ourselves to become patrons of a specific nation rather than fostering equal and positive relations with all nations. He warned us about a lot of things.

I don't suggest abandoning Israel by any stretch of the imagination, but in exchange for $3 billion annually, we should demand more for our money, and if they aren't willing to deal with their neighbors in a more appropriate manner, they are more than capable of defending themselves.

With the Arab spring, the nail is in the coffin for Iran's theocracy. It will take a long time for the Syrian rebels to over throw an entrenched military state, but once they do, Iran's only friend in the region will have been removed. Khameni has never had the charisma of his predecessor and it's only a matter of time before that system of government comes tumbling down.

Steve

April 22nd

My giant project to make an efficient turnover, is working well. This team is really big on turnover, and one of the things they said when they got here was that "turnover starts now." That means that they are preparing to leave the next team in good shape from the very beginning. That alleviates many of my complaints about the way we've fought this war.

April 24th

I completed the marathon today. Unfortunately, my running partner was needed as an extra crewmember on a convoy. I had intended on doing it as soon as my shift ended, but it was raining. After two hours of fitful sleep, I got out of bed and did the marathon, which took a little under four hours, over a hilly and rocky course that had to be repeated over and over again. It was a monotonous run with nothing special except for being in Afghanistan and something to pass the time.

April 26th

I saw a beautiful Indian Roller today. It's a brilliant blue and green bird that re-sembles an American Kingfisher in size and stature. I couldn't get to my camera in time for a picture. Robert took me on a tour of the towers, and I got to meet a lot of his security guards in addition to two new Pashtun interpreters who speak fantastic English, Dari, Pashto, and Urdu. They will be aiding Asad in his English classes. I also got to see some of the depressing side of nation building. Driving out to the tow-ers, we caught a soldier high-tailing it back from the tower after dropping off some pot for one of the stoner guards who just happened to be the Major's brother. Nepotism occurs in the west, but it's rare that it occurs in the military. Here, the Major had used his clout to ensure his brother got a security position locally. His brother had been caught sleeping on the job twice, and now he's getting stoned on the job from pot deliv-ered by a soldier for whom the towers are off limits. Baby steps …

I had a great time at dinner with the Uzbeks. Same meal: lamb stew with bread dipped in the juice. They also had some type of soup, but I didn't ask what was in it. These people always treat me with such a high regard. I really enjoy them.

April 27th

I wrecked my foot this afternoon. I was in mid-stride and swung it into an up-turned rock with a sharp point. I couldn't even walk back to base and caught a ride with a guy in an ATV. This is going to take a while to heal.

May 1st

I'm going to miss this place; that is all.

May 2nd

The poppies are blooming in full force. They are beautiful plants. Funny that I tried my best to grow crops, largely fail-ing, and poppies have sprung up outside my door without any help. I'm looking into harvest-ing some raw opium just for the hell of it. I might never have another chance. After the flower has finished blooming, it closes in on itself in order to produce the seeds. At some point, one scores the seedpod gently with a razor blade and a milky substance trickles out and dries into a paste. Afterwards, the dried paste is wiped off and collected and processed into heroin.

May 3th

I decided today is the day for my opium trip, as I will be leaving this installation tomorrow or the day after. I've waited until the last moment, because I don't know if I will experience any intense withdrawal that requires additional hits, so by insuring that I will not be able to readily get more, it will eliminate the possibility of a major addiction. That's my theory at least.

I had planned on scoring the poppies in the morning and sample them in the evening, but to my surprise, someone (probably Afghans) has already scored the bud. Someone is harvesting the poppies right here in our compound, which I find comical. Anyway, since there was already a copious amount of resin available on the poppy heads, I snapped off three and took them back to my room. I had no idea of the appropriate serving size of opium, so I decided to taste only a little bit at a time. Eating opium is less efficient than smoking it or making a tea, but I have limited options.

Immediately upon contact, the resin, which tastes like the pods of snap peas, numbs the tongue. The chemical is in the system relatively quickly, and the buzz was similar to that perfect amount of beer right before going over the top and drinking too much. Unlike beer, I perceived no loss of fine motor skills and twirled a pencil in my fingers as a test to see if I could. While testing my limitations, I continued to dab a little on my tongue and swallow in a piece-meal manner still not knowing how much was too much. Looking into the mirror, my pupils were more dilated than I imagined possible, but with the exception of slight irritation from the overhead lights, my eyesight remained unchanged. My heart rate, breathing, and hearing also remained unchanged, though my concentration while measuring my beats per minute seemed to fail me. Additionally, I lost complete sensation to extremities, face, and scalp despite maintaining muscle control. I gently chewed the remaining pods, but perceived no additional chemical. With my supply exhausted, I decided to go for a run. I did a few loops through the compound and at about 20 minutes, began to have hot flashes and shivering simultaneously. It was only about 70 degrees outside, but I was sweating. I finished the run and showered. By the time I showered, I could feel my scalp again, and by the time I was finished with a normal breakfast of a sausage patty, biscuit, and eggs, I was no longer shivering or sweating. I also had some Hershey's Kisses. I do not know the precise amount I consumed, but I would estimate it to be about the size of a pencil eraser. Obviously, it was enough for a brief high yet not enough to put me in a coma.

May 4th

I perceive no withdrawal today. I suspect I would have to use it repeatedly in order to become addicted, but I do not think the experience was a very good one, and I would not recommend it to anyone. Heroin is said to be better than sex. I haven't tried that, but I can safely say that opium is not better than sex.

I am done with my work here, and I am leaving on a convoy to Camp Bastion today.

May 5th

The convoy was delayed. I made it to Camp Bastion today, and I'll be going to Bagram sooner or later.

May 10th I was able to bypass KAF this time and come straight to BAF for some rudimentary out-processing. I should leave on the 12th.

May 15th
I'm out of here. After a few days of delays and being bumped from flights, I'm leaving Afghanistan. There really isn't anything else to say.

Bagram one year later

EPILOGUE

My time in Afghanistan was a mixture of positive and negative experiences.

Throughout my year in country, I maintained an optimism that was buoyed by what I observed around me—the words and actions of individual Afghans, and the perceptions I drew from the Americans with whom I worked. When it comes to the Afghans, I can admit that I often got an inaccurate portrayal of what life was really like in Afghanistan. As I dealt most often with Afghan Special Forces, I was dealing with the best and brightest that the "New Afghanistan" has to offer. While Afghanistan as a whole languishes as largely illiterate, almost all the Afghan soldiers I dealt with were literate in at least one language and often spoke rudimentary English after years of exposure to Americans. However, it was the Afghan laborers who gave me the most optimism. In so many of them was a fire to better themselves and to achieve more than their parents. It was expressed best by the Ali brothers and by the Rahman brothers, who demonstrated what investment in education really means—exponentially increasing education with the passing of each generation. When it came to Americans and their perception of the war, I often had to read between the lines in order to see the truth of our work in Afghanistan. Sadly, I felt compelled to ignore the largely irrelevant opinions of about two-thirds of the troops I interacted with. Many of them expressed either blind and unquestioning patriotism or jaded disdain marked by rhetorical questions of "why we are here?" as if 20 minutes on Wikipedia would not provide a suitable answer. Automatons and willfully ignorant people do us no good. However, among the remaining third of the troops was the cautious optimism of those who could see the marked improvement of our Afghan counterparts and accepted the loss of so many Americans as a necessary evil to prevent far more deaths in the long run should Afghanistan crumble into a non-functioning state and a host for extremists.

There were setbacks to my optimism. I met Afghans who loathed our presence and wanted us gone immediately. I met some whose paradigm was set so rigidly that they could see no value in learning new skills. Also, some students I lost to culture and laziness, unwilling to learn from an infidel. I took it personally when students stopped coming to class—not because of my own sense of self-importance but because

I truly believed that the tools I was offering were ones that would help, not just individual Afghans but the country as a whole. I took each coalition casualty and death personally and while I seldom mention my official duties in this publication, I met each day with ferocity to achieve as much as I could in my limited time. I was most angered by the attacks by Afghans wearing government uniforms. We will never know if these were Taliban sleepers waiting for the appropriate time to strike or merely attacks of opportunity by someone in a stolen uniform, but the damage done with each attack has been one of the biggest setbacks in the war. Finally, I took it personally when our own media actively undermined our efforts, not because of journalistic integrity, but be-cause of the rabid sensationalism that has endured since Vietnam and the Nixon ad-ministration. The media have a duty to question our government, but it must be done so in a productive manner. I find our current news sources to be severely wanting.

Even with all these setbacks, I remain optimistic to this day. Lashkar Gah, the capital city of Helmand, has remained relatively peaceful since its complete turnover to the Afghan Government in 2011. With nearly one-third of the total number of deaths in Afghanistan, the Helmand province is by far the most violent area in the country, but in Lashkar Gah, there has been no descent into anarchy, no sudden rash of suicide bombings or summary executions, and no wanton, retaliatory slaughter of Afghan civilians in our absence. I am not suggesting that absolutely no incidents have occurred in Lashkar Gah, I am aware that the Taliban are capable of luring us into a false sense of security, and I am certainly aware that the surrounding districts have yet to be completely calmed, but all in all, the Afghan government forces have demon-strated that they can hold that city. The question is, how to duplicate that success throughout the rest of Afghanistan.

The answer is time.

While the Afghan National Army has shown its capability, Afghanistan has only rudimentary air power that is insufficient to target the splinter groups that still plague the rural areas in Afghanistan. While the Afghan Intelligence Service is adept at find-ing out information locally, it lacks a holistic approach to intelligence and lacks the technology necessary for such an approach. Finally, there are areas still marred by a Taliban shadow government and to combat this threat, we need our Special Opera-tions Forces on the ground and continuing to expand the ALP and providing breathing room for locals who are continuing to build an Afghan economy.

ACKNOWLEDGEMENTS

Thanks to Andrea Billups, Kevin Simonson, Ted Spiker, Mike Foley, and William Mckeen for their continued instruction both in and out of the classroom.

Thanks to Brian Kim, Danny Paul, and all others whose enthusiasm pressed me to finish the book when I was questioning its worth.

Thanks to my ex-wife for being a sounding board while I was in Afghanistan

Thanks to Lauren for listening to me drone through the original draft as I stream-lined it for eventual publishing.

Thanks to Rebecca's Coffee on Juniper Street in San Diego for letting me take up hours of bandwidth while drinking only coffee.

Thanks to Sam Ronicker for volunteering to edit two drafts and aid in eventual production.

Thanks to the Afghans who shared their stories with me and gave me a picture of what life is like after years of war.

Thanks to the hundreds of thousands of coalition members who have given their time, their sweat, and their blood in this endless war. They have only died in vain if we refuse to learn from them.

One GIANT cellphone

ABOUT THE AUTHOR

I've known Steven for several years now, since our time at the language institute. He's always struck me as a free thinker, which is odd for the military, and I've always enjoyed that about him. We've shared many discussions about life, philosophy, religion, and politics, etc. all of which have helped to broaden my horizons. I've always felt he was destined for more than what the military had to offer. I'm proud of this work and I'm glad he solicited my help in making it a reality. I'm hoping that you enjoyed reading it as much as I enjoyed helping produce it

Samuel Ronicker, Editor

1 of 63

Made in the USA
Coppell, TX
09 July 2021